Echoes of Light

Jani Viswanath

PARTRIDGE

Cover design by Jani
Paradiso
Oil painting on canvas
Palette knife & blade
60x70 cms

Print information available on the last page.

To order additional copies of this book, contact
Partridge India
000 800 919 0634 (Call Free)
+91 000 80091 90634 (Outside India)
orders.india@partridgepublishing.com

www.partridgepublishing.com/india

To my parents who taught us the true meaning and dignity of compassion, selflessness and humanity;

Two beautiful souls I was blessed to share my journey with. Their light shines on long after they have left this mortal realm guiding every life they have touched and continues to shine from this world unto the next.

I truly believe that though you may be dead in one time zone, you are alive in another...

We love you eternally
Dr. T.K. Viswanath and Chandra Viswanath

My perspective

For the major part of my life, my father hammered one single thread of thought into my head.

He would say: "child, whatever you do, know the difference between ambition and greed. This is the fine line that separates the doer's and the damned. The reason why, we are at crossroads today is because we are losing the ability to sympathize and to empathize. We don't care or understand the difference between the two."

"and what is the difference?" I asked him.

"One is constructive and the other is destructive. One has a conscience, the other does not.

Ambition, is the desire to achieve something, to test the limits of your potential, to strive to do your best in whatever you choose to, and excel in it.

Greed, on the other hand, is a desire to hoard everything and to possess more than you need at any cost.

Ambition can be fulfilled. Unfortunately, greed cannot."

As the years rolled by, those words took on a deeper meaning.

Now, I remain forever in awe of our species. First, for the immense intellect, potential and perseverance we have and the heights we have reached from our very humble stone age beginnings, and Second, for our equally immense talent to self – destruct.

Intellectually superior we are, yes, but still unable to recognize the difference between the two.

Our destructive greed, self – obsession, petty politics, corrupt overwhelming capitalism and fanatic extremism are threatening to destroy the very fabric of the human race.

At the peak of our advancement, instead of mastering peaceful co – existence, here we are, still discussing peace, debating climate change and denying all other species their fair share of the planet.

We need to bring back and display a tiny bit of sensitivity that is the essential fabric of the human race and from which the word 'humane' originated.

The dire need of the moment is not how rich, or famous, or talented or gifted you are – but rather how kind and generous you are, how compassionate your actions are to the weak, poor and broken sections of society.

Being kind, being humane, this cannot be a trade or a barter. It has nothing to do with politics, business or religion. It is the fundamental duty of every conscientious, decent human.

Though I am born a Hindu Brahmin, having been educated in a catholic convent and spending a major part of my life in Muslim countries has made me realize one thing. At the point where our world is – my main religion is humanity and my God is compassion.

Beyond that, I do not have time to ponder who is right or wrong, where I fit in or where I don't, as there is so much to do. There are enough ever ready to hurt and abuse. It is time we heal.

Perhaps it would help us a great deal to go back to the basics; the simple rudimentary lessons needed for a comfortable, secure and happy society.

& so, I started to write, not about how to get rich or famous fast, not about how to get millions of views and followers on social media, not about how to reach the top or how to successfully manifest your dream love, job or house....

No, there are enough who can teach you how to get material success. I would be superfluous.

I write about emotions that are fast disappearing; I write about the invaluable treasures of basic humanity - kindness, inspiration and gratitude. The dignity of extending a hand to lift someone who has fallen down.

I write about the undervalued contentment of living in the present moment.

None of these costs much, yet they yield great results and fill us with hope and happiness.

The collection of stories and poems in this book reflect my emotions. Gliding back to a time when society, despite its myriad faults and weaknesses, was a bit simpler, a bit warmer (emotionally, not climatically) and a bit more trusting. People exhibited some decency, dignity and conscience.

My characters are flawed, yet they illustrate the joy of simple gestures, the power of kindness through ordinary actions, the magic of giving second chances to people who have erred.

The importance of utilizing our time by living in the present rather than chasing an uncertain future.

Nevertheless, we know this- that deep within, for the majority of us, a smile, a kind word and the joy of helping someone in need even in a small way is more rewarding than tastelessly exhibiting our vanity, our wealth, our privilege.

Compassion is what sets us apart from all other species – let's not lose it.

"Non est ad Astra Mollis e terris via"
There is no easy way from the earth to the stars

Lucius Annaeus Seneca

Contents

Poetry

Short Stories

Poetry

The spontaneous flow of raw emotion breathes life into words to give birth to an extraordinary being that knows not right or wrong and cares not for boundaries, flying high, disappearing into the horizon – free, liberated, alone…

Requiem

The Last Dance

Requiem is a remembrance, a ceremony for the departed. It may be a hymn, a chant or a musical piece performed in their honor. The word originates from Latin *requies*, which means rest.

Every religion and culture observe this practice in some form or other.

Requiem

Finally,
A moment of worth
A day of glory
How famed and fortunate am I?

The man of the hour
The guest of honor
The love and pride of all alike

Saluted, decorated, felicitated
The medal of bravery feted;
Commander of the operation
Returning from the war on invasion

What a magnificent setting
What a beautiful crowd!
Oh for a second, it made me so proud

I looked around for the cameras
TV crew, photographers, journalists, and some extras
All jostling to get a glimpse as I drove past

I looked at the crowd behind me … Did I know them?

My brain searched
Yes, famous faces all so pretty
Incredible, unknown to me, I had become a celebrity!

Did I miss something?
Not sure if I fit in with this glamorous crowd
I looked at myself
Though, daresay, I was well spruced out

Crisp and fresh, in full military attire
Medals pinned neatly for all to admire

Every guest there somehow was my best mate
I overheard some whisper
"What an admirable, brave, and gallant comrade!"

Serenaded with flowers, garland, bouquet and wreath
The variety—what a feast for the eye
Truly for their beauty, fragrance and rarity, they vie!

How lucky am I- to be loved so and admired
Was this my ultimate moment of splendor?
The pinnacle of my worth, I wondered!

I walked the red carpet, past adoring eyes
Flanked by the joint chief, the general, in full military
might

I glanced around as I walk past
My wife and young son were there as well?
Ah, but they looked aghast!

I must apologize to them later, I thought
Neither was a fan of pomp and protocol

We reached the podium, beautifully laid out
The military band, my favorite tune played out;
When they finished, we turned to position
Attention, salute, and the crowd roared in unison

The general said a few words to compliment
Acclaim, praise, commend;

My work, my life, my passion,
My valor, my sacrifice and dedication

Humbled and beholden
I rose to shake his hand
Fighting back the tears
That threatened to disobey my command...

He looked through me like I ceased to exist!
Looked straight ahead into the spectators' midst

Concluded his speech and stood to attention
The 21-gun salute went off in unison

I turned to the crowd;
Solemn and straight- they stood
Their eyes focused on the stage

I stepped closer, and there I was
With the most powerful people;
In the most beautiful setting

Peacefully asleep
In the most gorgeous, polished mahogany box...

Oh, what glory, what name?
A guest of honor indeed
What remarkable fame!

An honor did I care for?
A medal I had to die for

War—a symbol of a bad plot of a terrible drama
For mankind, totally uncalled for;

If I could turn back time
I would have cherished my prime
And not wasted time

Maybe a bit more of me
To my friends and family
A few precious moments
To my wife and son
Rather than my entire being
To a futile profession...

In the pursuit of eminence
The grandiose of nothingness;

We are but scavengers
Seeking acceptance

We *are* but characters playing different parts
In this gigantic theater called life, *not* just some art;
Some center stage, some minor roles, others just the extra

Races, nations, gender across all strata…

Little do we know
There's no one above or below
Who watches this unhinged show

I take my final *bow*, my friends

The ceremony is about to end
Melody of the final tune fades, my soul suspends

How sweet, how sublime

Requiem—the warmth of remembrance to a cold body
Requiem—the melody of sound to deaf ears
Requiem—the curtain disappears

Momentary darkness … and another door appears …

Wind Chimes and Waterfalls

So much has been written about love, which only proves that words fail to capture it completely. It is an enigma and always will be.

Love has been alive since the birth of the first dawn, in every living organism, but we try—without much success—to bend and sculpt it so that it fits within the confines of our limited intellect and understanding.

Wind Chimes and Waterfalls

What is love that the whole world raves about?
What is love;
But a vagabond child of the exuberant heart.

Drifting, wandering to quench its thirst—
Unaware, that momentary a drizzle,
And then mostly drought …

Like wind chimes and waterfalls,
Reborn—with every breeze and restless wave,

Yearning;

Only to ebb but for a while …
And arise again,
Your soul enslaved.

'Tis said that love is the entire universe within your heart,
A cosmic journey, when sparked;
Explodes with the force of a billion stars.

Love is the infinite depth of the ocean within,
Fascinating, enchanting, mesmerizing;
That dizzying vortex, it pulls you in.

Love is profound, it is ruthless, it is fierce;
Yet it is the only balm that soothes your wound,
And dries your tears.

Its fire can vanquish, burn, rage, and blaze,
While its winds gale, squall, devastate, and raze.

We try to lock, confine, define it in vain;
With our limited logic, frivolous guise, and disdain.

Love, that from the soul radiates -
Powerful and unabashed, it exhilarates.

Limitless, fearless, unapologetic;
Cares not who, why, how, or when—
It chooses to melt with, dissolve, and fuse into one.

Love was here long before we gave it a word,
In every cell, atom, and molecule of this world.

Is it
A passion, an emotion, an insatiable need?
Oh, why even try
To fathom?

Abstruse indeed ...

Void

Unfortunately, we are not conscious of our own mortality. If we truly comprehend and accept the fact that we are mortal and what matters is the joy and wisdom we leave behind, we will perhaps behave differently.

Void

Pause … Stop … Breathe …
Why are you running?
Where are you heading to?

The hustle, the bustle, this constant tussle!
The race to the moon, Mars, and beyond
In search of yonder worlds,
But,
Your own—forlorn.

Is it lack of prudence or plain conceit?
Striving to be the best—
Your manic urge to pass every test
To resist defeat.

Economic wars, military wars, chemical and biological
wars!
With reckless abandon it goes on …

Whence, why, for what?
Your rationale *foregone* …

Constant motion, ever increasing speed—
"Slow down," whispers the earth.
What a pity, no one pays heed …

"Slow down," whispers the earth;
For there is no need—
Running so hard is futile indeed …

Transient and irrelevant,
You are at best;
As the universe rumbles,
You fail your fundamental test.

Astounding, is it not?
Your intellect so slight
With greed, hate, and pretentious might.

I put you at the top, so you may well
Lead the way.
Cherish nature's treasures,
Instead—
You make life hell …

You fight so hard with everything around you—
Nature, my other children, and even with each other of you.
You can take nothing out of this orb, this sphere.
Oh, lest you forget—
Why, even your own body is leased to you
For a brief tenure.

The earth is round
No matter *what* you do.
Everything must come around.

And so all comes to an end;
You return to whence you came from, my friend.

Dust unto dust—a tiny particle that's all.
Greed, vanity, fame, and fortune—

Oh what?

It's all but a heady spin before a hollow fall ...

Journey

Life has no pre-written scripts, no re-takes & no awards when you finish, the biggest reward being every moment lived well & complete.

Journey

And for all those who fear loneliness,
What do they know?
Of love and peace and harmony
That, in the utter silence of one's presence, grow.

Gliding along the moonlit path,
The wind and the trees serenade
Their unconditional love
With beauty and effortless grace.

The breeze kisses me softly; she whispers,
"Set your mind free from the shackles of this world;
They breed pain.
Humankind has become fickle, selfish, greedy, and vain."

I look up at the silver moon, lazily awake.
She casts aside the blanket of clouds,
Unveiling her radiant face.
Beautiful, bewitching, and sublime, she captivates.

I look at her beauty, dazed!
She smiles at me and accentuates.
"There's no parallel to me," she says.

"The universe works in synchrony.
The stars, the planets, I—
We are in complete harmony.

"The sun gives me his energy that I may
Shine upon the earth at night when he is away.
Can you, for a moment, imagine?" she asks?

Were we to fight,
What then would be your plight?

Why do you not realize
That war and blood is a useless sacrifice?

Look at us and learn,
Uninterrupted, Unhindered yet in
Unison we govern.

The rivers, the seas, the valleys, and the mountains,
Cherish these gifts this earth has given.
There is no other planet so benevolent
Like this earth that you so callously abandon.

Nostalgia

Memories are the only force you can carry with you anytime, anywhere; and the best part of it is, good, bad, or indifferent, *you* get to make them. It's in your hands alone.

Nostalgia

Standing at the crossroads of life,
I take a few minutes to pause and ponder;
Lest I race ahead without realizing that my journey has
come to an end.

Nostalgia—a wonderful feeling of pleasure and pain.

I look back at the path long traveled, with its sharp curves
and bends.
The journey—exciting, eventful, and every inch as
memorable.

What a world it was growing up!

A world of basic needs and simple pleasures,
Carefree thoughts, and beautiful gestures.
Those were the days of ghosts and goblins,
Of fairy tales and fables.

Waking up to a foggy morning,
Gleefully
Examining the dewdrops on petals.

Those were the days of picnic baskets and jolly cheer,
Innocent pranks, mischief, and ice-cold beer.

Covert glances aching to meet and
Stolen kisses behind the trees

Waiting for the milkman to bring fresh milk and
The postman to deliver a letter from a loved one's ilk.

Helping your neighbor fix a leaking roof;
The whole street making fresh rolls and hot soup
When you had the flu.

Those were the days of unrestrained giggles and laughter,
Of children playing on the streets without worry or fear,
Your neighbor overseeing your kids while you leave on
an urgent errand,
Or those times when you cheered for your neighbor's son
at school or clapped for his band.

Those were the days when lovers quarreled and
Longed to make up with a kiss and a rose;
When your whole office celebrated your birthday, your
wedding,
Or shared your sorrows.

Those were indeed the days when strangers cared,
Stopped to help, push your car, or carry your bags;

When friends were family
Who woke up at night hastily
To take your daughter to the doctor or
Pick you up from an airport on the city border.

Yes indeed—those were the good old days.
The good old happy days when people had time for each other …
Wonder where they have withered.

I look ahead, and I now see
A mindless, frantic buzz of energy.

People hurrying and scurrying past,
Glazed eyes skimming over.

Muttering on their phones and checking the zillion apps,
Young and old alike, never mind the age gap!

Incessant talk, robotic walk, virtual thrills;
Lonely hearts, vacuous lives, dissatisfied still,

A hug, a smile—the human touch has been killed.
I let out a slow, long breath and walk on as I taste the tears on my lips.

Tears of happiness.
To have seen the old world of bliss
And tears of sadness for future kids
Who will never know what they have missed.

Yes, nostalgia—a wonderful feeling of pleasure and pain.

Short Stories

Long ago, during one of my visits to a remote village in Kenya, a group of children gathered around me. I gave them some sweets and they still lingered around. I asked them what else they wanted. One of the boys mustered up some courage and asked me, "can you tell us a story please?"

I smiled and agreed.

I was not a great storyteller, but the excitement on their faces gave me the confidence and the reason to begin...

Sinners and Saviors

"A kind word, a caring gesture, a compassionate heart and a willingness to listen can turn a life around".

Sinners and Saviors

It was almost six weeks since the lockdown began. The garment factory was shut, and Ivan had lost his job. He worked as a sorter in the finishing department. His job was to check each garment thoroughly for small defects before sending it for final packing.

The factory he worked in was on the border of Bandung, the third largest city in Indonesia. Located above sea level, the city is cool and lies on a river basin surrounded by volcanic mountains.

Ivan lived in a small village called Cipageran in north Cimahi on the outskirts of Bandung. It was a poor neighborhood. Most people who lived there were factory labor or daily-wage workers. The houses were run-down, crammed, and dingy sheds.

Ivan lived in a tiny, tiled roof and brick walled house. Paint was rapidly peeling off what used to be a cobalt blue color. The once red tiles on the roof had turned a smoky brown and black due to exposure to the sun and the rains, which is typical of Bandung weather.

They used lanterns, as electricity was always a problem. The dim yellow bulbs that hung precariously from the ceiling were no better than the lanterns anyway.

Ivan lived with his parents and older sister Widya. He had a six-year-old niece whom he absolutely adored.

The little girl, Ira, loved him as he was the only father figure she knew. He had been close to his sister till she met Ronnie, a good-for-nothing freeloader.

Widya fell in love with the useless bloke when she was nineteen, and after just four months of dating him, she got pregnant. The rascal left her and ran the minute he knew she was pregnant. No one heard from him since that day. Widya decided to keep the child instead of having an abortion. Ira turned out to be the biggest blessing in the gloomy household.

Life was tough. Ivan's meager savings dried out long ago. He was living on small, borrowed sums from friends, barely enough to bring home a bit of food for his parents and niece. His sister was hardly ever home. He did not see her for days on end. They had no idea where she went or what she did.

Ivan and his mother played the role of parents to Ira. He knew that at some point, he would have to have a serious talk with his sister.

But for now, there were other more pressing problems on his mind—survival for instance!

Without a job, he couldn't borrow any more money from his friends. They didn't have much to lend anyway.

The virus thing looked bad everywhere. The TV news was all about how this flu killed people. He couldn't understand why everyone made such a big deal about it. It was just a flu. It was not like the earth was being attacked by aliens. He had seen in the news that many big countries had imposed curfew and people couldn't go out. But then, the *bules* (foreigner) were afraid of everything.

Bandung had no curfew. A few cautious people covered their face with scarves or masks. Ivan joked with his friends that no virus could last as the people were so immune to everything. The food they ate, the dust, and the living conditions were all worse than the virus.

Ivan had come to meet his best friend, Agus, who worked with him at the factory. Agus was from a family of cooks. They were from West Sumatra from the Minang tribe. His father was a great cook who had the most popular Padang food stall in Jakarta, but he had an unfortunate accident and lost his left hand and his business.

Jalan Braga used to be a bustling place lined with many street hawkers and vendors on carts full of various types of delicious food. The place was a famous attraction for locals and tourists alike.

Ivan looked around. *Might as well have been a lockdown here too,* he thought. The Tokos and *rumah makan* (shops and cafés) were almost empty. People had no money as the factories were closed.

Ivan's thoughts were cut off as he heard Agus. "Hey, Ivan, so long, bro, how have you been?"

He saw Agus parking his scooter and went over to him. "Good to see you again, Agus." He smiled, slapping his friend on the back".

They sat on the side of the pavement and shared a plate of Padang food between them.

"Ah, how I have missed this," said Agus, biting into a chunk of pork. "Ivan, you and I, we would be great cooks. If only we had a stall," he lamented, mixing the coconut and chili gravy into the rice.

This hawker had the best Padang food in the whole street, and he was always busy, but even he seemed to have few customers. Sitting on the side of the pavement, smoking Gudang Garam after dinner and catching up was heaven.

Agus seemed to know a lot about everything. He said the virus came from China and spread all over the world. He felt the Chinese wanted to infect the whole world so they could take over. They already had a cure or vaccine or whatever they call it but wanted to release it only when more people were infected in the world so they could make money. It seemed like a reasonable theory to Ivan.

"Can't put anything past these selfish Chinese bastards," Ivan mused.

The Chinese were capable of anything. Most business owners in Bandung were Chinese, and they were not nice. They were aloof and cold, not to mention stingy!

The Chinese were hard taskmasters and paid very little. Even that had dried out, as most laborers lost their jobs and the factories did not want to pay them for sitting at home.

Ivan's eyes glinted as an idea began to form in his head. "Since we are in this deep shit because of these Chinese bastards, why don't we make them pay for it?"

Agus squinted, his small eyes disappearing to slits. He looked at Ivan lazily, his cigarette dangling from the corner of his mouth. "Ya, Ivan, and how do we do that. Rob them at gunpoint?" he asked sarcastically.

Ivan paused for a few seconds and, slowly releasing a ring of smoke from his lips, said, "Exactly. Let's rob one of them, but not at gunpoint."

Agus looked stunned. His cigarette dangled precariously between his lips and fell to the ground. He hurriedly picked it up and puffed on it vigorously a few times.

Finally, after a long minute, he said, "You are crazy, Ivan. If we get caught, we won't see open skies for a long time."

"Agus, look, what do we have to lose? No job, no money, nothing. We will die of starvation anyway. If we manage to rob something, we can provide for our families. So what if we get caught and end up in jail after that? And by the way, we get free food in prison, bro, heh?"

Agus did not like his joke and glared at Ivan, but he egged on, "It's not like we will get a job anywhere soon. What option do we have?"

Agus looked uncertain. He seemed like he wanted to do it but was afraid of getting caught. He paced the street up and down while Ivan gazed at a kid's dress at the shop window opposite them, wishfully wondering if he would ever be able to buy it for his niece.

Ivan realized that if he pushed Agus a bit, he would buckle. "Look, bro, if we get caught, I will say it was all my idea and I forced you into it, okay?"

Finally, after what seemed an eternity, Agus looked at Ivan, flicked his finger, and said, "Come on, bro. If you go down, I go down … Okay, let's do it. What's your plan?"

Ivan paused. "Let's go to the residential area of our boss, Pa Chung—"

Agus cut in, baffled. "Ivan, that is the craziest idea I have heard. You *bodo* [fool], you want to rob our boss?! He knows our entire background, might as well go to the cops now and surrender."

"I haven't finished," said Ivan, a bit irate. "I have delivered parcels from the factory to Pa Chung's home. There is a house at the end of the lane where an old Chinese couple live. I have seen them having tea alone on the veranda many times. I never saw anyone else around. They are an easy target for us."

Agus looked a bit queasy. "I am not robbing an old couple, Ivan, forget it," he protested.

Ivan countered emphatically. "Agus, think, bro," he said, jabbing a finger at his temple. "It's the easiest way. No one is going to get hurt. We won't hurt them. We will just go in, tie them up, take some things, and leave. Maybe they have rich kids so they won't feel the loss of anything, okay?"

After an hour of cajoling, Agus finally agreed.

They started making plans. Agus had a friend, Agung, who ran a small transport business. His business was also struggling. They decided to borrow the van from him. Agus promised that he would pay him the moment they got paid. Having no money, Ivan pleaded with him to fill up the gas. Agung looked at them with pity, shook his head and warned Agus to be careful with the van.

The job was planned for Thursday night, a quiet day before the noisy weekends.

Ivan was to ring the doorbell, pose as an employee from the electricity department, and ask to check the electrical DB. He would then tie up the couple and get away with whatever he could find. Agus would wait at the end of the road and give him exactly five minutes before coming to the main gate of the house to help move the stuff into the van and escape.

The plan was sound, yet the night before, Ivan tossed and turned on his wobbly cot. Shafts of moonlight streamed through cracks in the tiled roof, washing the tiny room of the brick-walled house his father had built with an ethereal glow.

He saw the figures of his old parents curled on a hard mattress on the floor. They were simple, God-fearing people. They would die of shock were they to know of their son's intentions.

Kota Baru Parahyangan, where Pa Chung, lived was a tony neighborhood on the outskirts of Bandung. A gated community with rows of two-story houses flaunting neat front and back lawns, it was home to mostly Chinese businessmen and some wealthy Indonesians.

At eight on Thursday evening, Ivan and Agus dressed in overalls and drove up to the main gate of the expansive residential complex.

"Apa kabar pa? Semua baik?" (How are you, sir? All well) Ivan waved at the two security guards and held up a parcel bearing the address of their former employer.

"Ya pa, baik baik saja." (Yes, sir, all okay, okay.) One of them waved back. The big iron grilles flung open, and the van wheeled in.

"What if the guards get suspicious?" Agus hissed, wiping the sweat off his forehead. "We will work something out with them from the cash we get. They don't carry firearms, and the worst they can do is beat us with their batons and call the cops," Ivan said calmly.

They circled the complex. The houses were located wide apart and the vicinity was mostly quiet. They crossed the residence of Pa Chung and stopped at the end of the lane where the old couple lived. A dim yellow bulb lit the front porch. All the curtains were drawn. A light shone through the curtains upstairs and a soft light gleamed faintly through the curtains on the ground floor.

There was a small park opposite the house surrounded by a cluster of trees. A few benches, a swing, and an exercise frame were randomly placed at one end of the park. Agus parked the van. Ivan jumped down and signaled Agus with a thumbs-up and a five.

The small wrought iron gate was unlocked. Ivan opened it and walked to the front door. Taking a deep breath, he rang the bell and waited anxiously for what seemed like eternity. Finally, he could hear the slow shuffle of feet. A small, frail old man opened the door and squinted at Ivan through his glasses.

"*Permisi bapak* [sir], I am from the electric department, I have to check your DB board. A technical problem has been reported from this area," stated Ivan, forcing a smile.

The old man let him in and escorted Ivan to the DB board, which was to the end of the hall near the kitchen. He shuffled back to his seat in front of the TV.

Ivan pretended to check some switches in the DB board while scanning the surroundings. It was a tidy, pretty house. Just then, he heard an old woman's voice from the kitchen, "Who is it, Wang?"

"Just the electrical boy checking something," shouted the old man from the hall.

Will tie up the old man first and then handle the old lady, decided Ivan. He removed a knife and rope from the pocket of his overalls and walked to where the old man sat, knife in one hand and rope in the other.

Ivan heard the old woman's voice again, "Son, have some tea and cake after you are done, I am making a fresh cup for you."

Ivan paused for a second, and his heart jumped.

"How can you hurt these nice old people," a tiny voice in his head taunted as he quickly pushed it away. *No one was going to get hurt anyway,* he reasoned.

The old man was sitting with his back to Ivan. *Easier than anticipated,* he thought as he stood behind the old man and inhaled sharply.

"Son, sit down, my wife is making tea for ..." The old man trailed off and paled seeing the knife in Ivan's hand.

"*Bapak* [sir], I won't hurt you. Please do as I say, don't make any noise, and we will all be fine." muttered Ivan.

The old man was quiet, and his face had regained its composure. He had a strong yet gentle face. He looked like someone who had seen too much in life to be frightened easily. Ivan looked into his eyes briefly, unnerved by the kindness and warmth in them.

Ivan tied the old man's frail, wrinkly hands and feet as gently as he could. The old man's eyes never left Ivan's face, following every move minutely.

His wife walked in with a small tray of tea and cake. Ivan's back was to her as he hunched on his knees, facing the old man so she could not see what he was doing. She kept the tray on the table, picked the cup of tea, and held it to Ivan. "Here you go, son, this cake is delicious. You can take some home too."

As Ivan turned, the old lady took in the scene—her husband tied up, the rope, the knife. Her face paled. The teacup rattled in her hand, but she managed to put it back on the table. She sat on the chair next to her husband.

"I suppose you want to tie me up too," she said feebly, offering her frail hands to Ivan.

The old man was silent.

What is with this couple? he was disconcerted. No drama, no noise—just a calm, dignified poise. *How I hate myself,* thought Ivan.

Ivan felt ashamed and embarrassed. Fighting the tears that welled up, he cursed his fate. *How can I be so foolish and heartless? I have never hurt anyone in my entire life, and here I am robbing a kind, defenseless old couple.* Ivan clenched his teeth to stop his tears.

As the unruly tears rolled down his face, the old man saw them. He looked at Ivan gently and whispered, "Take what you have to. You don't need to tie up my wife. She is old and weak and can do no harm."

Ivan got up from the floor and went to her chair. She sat quietly, a small, frail woman with a lot of dignity. She too had a kind face that had the stamp of generosity all over it. As she looked up at Ivan and saw the tears, she looked away perplexed, not knowing what to do.

At that moment, Agus stormed in and took in the entire scene. He rushed over to Ivan. "Here, I will tie her up, you go and get the stuff."

As he was about to grab her hands, Ivan hissed, "Don't touch her. She won't do anything."

Agus looked at Ivan puzzled, shook his head, and started collecting the things in the room. There were a couple of watches, a phone, a clock, a few silver pieces, a TV, and a DVD player.

They took everything portable and left the TV, as it would attract attention. Ivan asked the old man for his wallet. He pointed to the bedroom.

Ivan dashed in and saw the wallet on the dressing table. Inside was 1 million rupiah ($100) along with some credit cards. He took the money and left the wallet behind. He did not want to get into the credit card mess. He searched the drawers and found an envelope under the clothes. He quickly opened and glanced at the wad of cash inside. Pleased, he took it and ran back to the living room.

Agus had almost finished loading the van. He returned and checked. "All done, nothing else to carry?"

Ivan nodded, and Agus signaled him to leave.

As Ivan headed toward the door, he turned to the old couple. The old woman's hands were tied up, and she sat silently next to her husband. He turned to Agus angrily. "What the hell did you do that for? I told you to leave her alone."

"Better be safe than sorry, bro. You will thank me later. I will wait in the van," snapped Agus.

Ivan looked at the old couple and folded his hands. "Please forgive me. I have no choice but to resort to this. My family needs my support. I lost my job and haven't been able to find another. I am so sorry."

At that very moment, Ivan heard the sound of a baby's cries. The crying got louder. He looked toward the stairs and then at the old man quizzically. "I had no idea there was someone at home. Who else is upstairs?" Ivan asked nervously.

"My grandson. He must have woken up from his sleep. His parents should be home soon," replied the old man calmly.

Ivan's stomach twisted into a knot. There was not a second to be wasted, but there was no way he could leave without knowing the baby was fine.

He bolted up the stairs and saw the baby in the bedroom. The poor thing was almost choking in his tears, banging his little hands on the side of the crib.

Ivan went over and picked up the baby gently. He was wet and probably hungry. His tiny little hand was bleeding a bit.

Ivan picked up a blanket and towel from the crib and rushed downstairs with the baby. He placed the baby gently on the couch and asked the old man where the feeding bottle was, realizing it would take too much time to untie the old woman to feed the baby.

The old man pointed to the kitchen and said, "In the warmer."

There was a small gadget that was plugged in with some feeding bottles in it. The milk was warm. Ivan picked up one bottle and rushed back to the howling baby. He removed his wet clothes and wrapped him in the dry blanket. Ivan had plenty of experience in this area having taken care of his niece all by himself.

Ivan gently fed the baby, who quickly calmed down once he slurped the milk.

The old man observed every move of Ivan's and took in his actions with a mixture of relief and sadness.

Agus stormed in at this point to see what was causing the delay and took in the whole scene with incredulity. His eyes went wide with disbelief.

"Ivan, you are fucking mad, you need mental help! What the fuck are you feeding the baby for, you retard?! There is a car approaching."

Ivan waved him away. "A minute, the baby is almost fed."

Agus growled. "No, you idiot. You better leave, I will wait exactly for one minute." And he stormed off.

Within seconds, the door swung open, a young couple walked in and froze. Their parents were tied up, and a stranger was feeding their baby. It was a scene that could not even be written about in a film.

"I am calling the police. Back off right now," the lady in high heels squeaked, while her husband fumbled in his pocket for the phone.

Before Ivan could say anything, the old man interjected, "Keep the phone away, Lin." And he turned to his son. "Both of you, calm down. Everything is fine. Let the boy go." The young couple, though bewildered, obeyed him.

The old man looked at Ivan gently. "Son, leave the baby on the couch and go. Get your life sorted. You are a good boy. Don't fall into this pit of darkness. Crime will take you down a deep, dark hole you can never get out of."

Ivan placed the feeding bottle next to the baby and apologized to the old woman for his friend's brusqueness. Then he cupped the old man's tied hands and whispered, "You are an angel," and darted out.

Down the road, Agus was still waiting, fidgeting uncontrollably as Ivan ran to the van. The moment he jumped in, Agus went ballistic. "What the fuck were you thinking, you moron! Do you have a death wish or what? I thought they must have held you. One second more and I would have left. What the hell happened in there?"

On the drive back, Ivan told him the whole story. His voice broke and Agus glanced at Ivan sideways. He could see Ivan trying to hold back his tears.

"This is not the path I want to take in life, Agus," he sobbed. Agus looked at him distraught.

"Ivan, let it be now. We can't undo it. At least we didn't harm anyone, right? We will figure out a more decent way to live, I promise brother."

Ivan looked at his childhood friend. He was not a bad guy. A bit rough around the edges, but his heart was in the right place.

Ivan made a promise to himself. *I will repay the kindness and faith the old man showed me. No matter what destiny has in store for me, I will control my choices. No more stealing or cheating. Even if I have to clean the bins on the street, I will do it with dignity.*

Ivan flirted with the idea of giving the stolen goods back, but Agus wouldn't hear of it.

"The old man let you go, Ivan. He understood your situation and told you to take care of your family, and that is what we will do. We will turn our life around and will thank him in some way," he assured.

They sold the stolen goods at a pawn shop, and along with the cash they had stolen, they had about 40 million rupiah ($4,000), enough to help their families and start afresh.

A new Padang food kiosk opened near the bus stand on Jalan Braga, the most popular street in Bandung. The boys named it after the old man.

The reputation of Pa Wang Padang *toko* and of its owners as decent, principled, and kind people grew, and even the customers treated them with respect.

Two young, talented cooks became the rage. They served food with passion and enthusiasm. Ivan reveled in seeing customers enjoy the taste of their cuisine. The fire crackled under frying pans and large vessels sizzled, stewing thick gravies, while people huddled around for takeaways or to grab a bite by the sidewalk. A bench was kept on the side for women and kids.

It was almost five months since the incident. Agus and Ivan worked a grinding routine starting at five thirty every morning to set up and prepare for breakfast time. They served food till almost midnight every day. The only break they had was to take turns for a smoke or the bathroom.

Toward the end of the night, Ivan regularly kept more than two dozen food packets aside to give away free. Every night before closing the kiosk, the road cleaners, rag pickers, and garbage cleaners would come to Pa Wang's to take their food packets home.

This routine had started on the first week of opening when a garbage cleaner bought a plate of food and requested Ivan to let him take an extra packet of food home for his parents, and pay for it the next day. Ivan gave him both packets and said it was a gift. The garbage cleaner wept with happiness as he thanked Ivan.

For some inexplicable reason, the cleaner's joy and relief gave Ivan immense happiness. From that night, Ivan decided that they would give away free food parcels to the cleaners and homeless people.

It wasn't hard to convince Agus, who agreed instantly. The word spread quickly. Every night, the cleaners, the rag pickers, and the homeless would wait patiently for Ivan and Agus to serve the last paying customer, after which Ivan would signal to them to collect their free food parcels; and every night, each one of these destitute souls would shower them with blessings.

This was also the time of night Ivan looked forward to the most.

Soon, Pa Wang's became the most desired hot spot in the area, and ten months into their new beginnings, they were all set to open a second branch on the parallel street to cope with the demand.

Agus and Ivan, two stupid, irrelevant, reckless blokes, were fortunate to be given a second chance at life. Beneath the layers of desperation and helplessness in their petty act of crime, the old man saw two lost young adults worth rehabilitation.

Living angel is what Ivan called Pa Wang—the old man. His magic touch had brought out the goodness in both of them, now ever willing to step up for the deprived and the destitute.

The Storyteller of Baghdad

My English professor once said, "When you leave this world, the light at the end is not about how wealthy or accomplished you are. It is only about who you have lifted up in their darkest hour and whose life has changed for the better because of you."

The Storyteller
of Baghdad

I work as an evaluator at the Royal Academy of Arts
in London. At the risk of sounding vain, I may add, that
my passion for art combined with an uncanny talent for
recognizing an original from the best of reproductions
gave me an edge over most curators.

I was well respected and quickly rose to become one
of the chief advisors on the panel for the Committee of
Evaluation for established and emerging artists. At twenty-
nine, I was the youngest co-chair of the department,
assisting Chris, a British guy double my age.

The grapevine had it that the academy planned to trim
staff at the top due to a fund crisis. It was widely rumored
that the management would keep me and let Chris go,
as they wanted to have young talent to cope with the
emerging times.

Chris was getting nervous and anxious with every
passing day, even though no official announcement was

made. He had three teenage kids and a mortgage. I could understand his plight. One afternoon over lunch, Chris talked to me about his fear of losing his job and how difficult it would be for him to cope. There was nothing I could say to make him feel better. It wasn't my decision. I listened to him patiently, assuring him that we would talk on my return from my holidays.

Kuwait hadn't changed a bit since my last visit two years ago. My parents had asked me to spend a few days with them during the Eid holidays and since there was nothing much happening at the office I decided to visit them.

My father was posted as a diplomat for the India embassy in Kuwait after his tenure in Iran. Having spent most of my childhood in the Middle East, I knew the region and the language well.

My parents were thrilled to see me. Though I was close to both of them, my mother indulged me more. She visited me twice a year ever since I moved to London four years back.

Glimpses of the sandy roads, mosques and minarets on the drive home from the airport brought back wonderful memories. The Muezzin's call for prayer stirred old emotions as I closed my eyes and recalled my love for this rustic place.

The Middle East is a surreal place. It carries an exotic appeal and life is so much simpler than the West.

Having traveled throughout the Middle East and Africa on various occasions, I am awed by their magnetic charm and mystic aura that I find difficult to put into words. Only those who have lived here would truly understand its magic.

Wherever you visit—be it Jordan, Turkey, Lebanon, UAE, or Iraq—they have this wonderful otherworldly feel reminiscent of the old days of the Persian Empire. One could be forgiven for slipping into a time capsule and being transported to another bygone era just by walking into the *souks*, or night markets, in Damascus or Baghdad.

The narrow streets and alleyways littered with endless variety of colorful shops sell everything under the sun. Antique teapots and urns, carpets and silks, spices and honey—you name it and it appears!

As you walk through the enchanting lanes, the hypnotic fragrance of oud and attar wafting from tiny shops calm your senses instantly.

The vibrant shisha shops in the by-lanes beckon you and as you close your eyes, you could easily imagine the place being a perfect setting for Aladdin and his genie or Scheherazade's 1,001 Arabian nights.

Ah, how I loved and hated the active lethargy of this place!

I reached home to an excited mother who expressed her love the way only Indian mothers can. By feeding me as if I had been stranded in a jungle for years. At some point during lunch, as I prattled about life in London, she told me that we were going to visit our friends in Baghdad the following weekend.

The drive to Baghdad from Kuwait was unforgettable. We passed a group of Bedouins on a caravan of camels shuffling along the long stretch of undulating desert. We stopped by a roadside cafés to savor delicious shawarmas, falafels and kadak chai and the warm chat I had with the old owner about his family's Eid celebrations reminded me of the bland, apathetic life I had in London.

The city of Baghdad spawns on both sides of the Tigris River, the east bank and the west bank. The east bank is known as Al Rusafah, and the west bank as Al-Karkh. The east end of the city is home to a low-income district mainly inhabiting the Shia community.

On the west bank are residences for wealthy upper middle- and upper-class communities.

A series of bridges and a railroad connects the two banks. The main center and financial district originally used to be the Rashid Street in Baghdad hosting upmarket boutiques, cafés, and restaurants that lined the beautiful promenades. But in the nineties, it became an exclusive residential area due to its strategic location, being directly opposite the presidential palace across the Tigris.

We had planned to stay with my father's friend, Farid, for a few days. He was an affluent businessman originally from Jordan, married to a lovely lady from Brazil.

When he was in Kuwait a few years ago, he met my father at an embassy function. They hit it off and have been great friends ever since. Their friendship was one of mutual love and respect.

Uncle Farid, as I like to call him, lived in an affluent upper-class neighborhood called Al Mansur, along the race track on the west bank. The community had walled villas and gardens, branded boutiques, sidewalks, and cafés. There was ample security around.

Theirs was a beautiful Moroccan-style villa with a huge garden in front and a pool at the back.

Rehaan, their son, was a year older than me and a good friend. He had joined his dad's business.

They were at the porch to receive us. Rehaan, a tall, handsome young man with chiseled features, sprinted to the gate as soon as he saw us drive in and greeted me with a bear hug.

Uncle Farid almost crushed me with his hug. "Kian my boy, you have grown more handsome than I remember." He guffawed with a hard slap on my back as I smiled sheepishly.

After freshening up, we came down for drinks. Uncle Farid was a man who loved the arts, music, and theater. He probably had the best collection of records and classic films in the country.

Enchanting music flowed from the living room, infusing an air of tranquility. It was a piece I recognized from the German philharmonic orchestra—yes, Pavane by Gabriel Fauré, the famous French composer, pianist, and teacher.

We had a few drinks and caught up with our ends of the world. Uncle Farid, curious to know what I thought of London, asked Rehaan if he wanted to go there. Rehaan had no interest in Europe or the West. His heart belonged here.

Our mothers joined us a bit before dinner. It was a sumptuous, elaborate spread enough to feed an army.

Post - dinner, Rehaan asked me if I had ever been to a storytelling night.

I looked at him perplexed. My expression said it all. I laughed and said, "The only storytelling I recollect must have been when I was about twelve years old. One evening, after a family dinner, my father gathered all my cousins and promised an exceptional story. He proceeded to narrate it with gusto. He forgot the plot halfway and finished with a totally different plot than the one he started with. From that day, we avoid him and any form of storytelling." Rehaan laughed.

"Hakawati is a traditional storyteller," continued Rehaan. "Throughout the month of Ramadan, every night, there is a storytelling evening at the tent in the square. It will be an experience you won't forget, Kian. They only start after 10:30 p.m., so let's go."

It was just 9:00 p.m. My dad was enjoying his Cuban cigar and engrossed in Uncle Farid's new record collection. I just waved to him and left.

We drove out to the edge of the town along the Tigris. The entire city sparkled in white and gold like a magical kingdom. Trees, buildings, street lamps were all beautifully lit with strings of fairy lights to celebrate Eid.

We reached the Ramadan tent at the heart of the old city. It was a fairly large, luxurious setup.

The moment I walked in; I was transported to another world. Beautiful Moroccan stained-glass chandeliers hung from the ceiling reflecting soft hues in various colors of the rainbow, giving the room an ethereal feeling.

The floor was covered with soft Persian rugs and carpets. Small round tables were filled with plates of dates, Turkish cookies, and sweets. Waiters moved around offering Turkish coffee in tiny cups from antique gold-rimmed pots.

The seating was old traditional majlis style—cushions strewn around on the floor. Though the tent was quite busy, it was designed in a spacious manner. Soft Arabic music filled the air.

The audience was a mix of women and men of all ages. A few foreigners arrived with their native friends. I was intrigued to see large groups of women dressed in abayas and kaftans, some smoking shishas. The diverse mix of nationalities reflected well on the storyteller's popularity.

Perhaps in some way, all of us yearn to feel, to experience, a bit of history wherever and however we can find it. Holding on to the past connects us to the roots of our culture and civilization.

Rehaan and I selected a nice corner close to the stage and poured ourselves some Turkish coffee. The sweets richly sprinkled with nuts were delicious. We leaned back, relaxed, and waited for the Hakawati to arrive.

The fragrances wafting from oud and incense sticks combined with the soft clang of kava cups were soothing, lifting my spirits.

A slightly elevated podium stood in the center of the tent decorated with beautiful rugs and cushions. A small table held water and dates.

At about ten twenty, a tall, regal-looking man dressed in a rich, embroidered kaftan and a turban walked in, flanked by two lackeys.

He had a handsome chiseled face with an aquiline nose and a sharp jaw. His closely trimmed beard accentuated his perfect jawline.

He took long, graceful strides and prepared to sit down at the center of the stage. His lackeys quickly adjusted his cushions to ensure he was comfortable. One of them reverently poured a glass of water as he signaled them to leave.

His gaze swept the hall. As the soft light fell on him, his striking eyes held the crowd. He had magnetic, deep, black eyes that seemed to glow from within.

He adjusted the mic and, placing his hand on his heart, said in a deep voice, "A salaam a'lekum Shukran lajaeal hdha almasa' khasa." (Greetings and thank you for making this evening special.) He added in excellent English, "It's a pleasure to be here with all of you."

His voice was hypnotic, and I was beginning to understand why he was considered such a famous storyteller.

The Hakawati looked like a character out of the Arabian nights—regal and mysterious. His demeanor added to the aesthetics and transported time to another century.

He continued, "Storytelling has been a part of many cultures for centuries. People would gather around after dinner at the town square, the village, or even the front yard to listen to stories and poems retold by seers or more knowledgeable men.

"These stories from far-off lands and different cultures were exotic to listen to, but more often than not, they had a lesson in them. Some piece of wisdom you could go home with. Storytelling would typically start after dinner and continue through the night into the wee hours of dawn.

"When I tell stories in the village, you can see the mist at the first light of dawn by the time I finish and the villagers still want more." He laughed. "How many of you want to sit here till dawn?" He chuckled.

"Yes, we all do," the crowd chorused.

Smiling, he continued, "In the old days, storytelling was an event that brought people together. It was a means of social interaction to meet and talk, in towns and villages. Now, you have concerts." He smiled.

A group of teens in the far corner sniggered and laughed. The Hakawati paused, looked at them, and asked if they had something to say. One of the teens said, "Looks like an awful waste of time by the whole town, sir."

The Hakawati stared at them intently for a few seconds. The teens started fidgeting uncomfortably. "Son, people in the old days did not wile away the whole day storytelling. They had discipline and a time for everything. They worked hard from dawn to dusk. On weekends, they would meet, not just to listen to stories but to each other as well. The community was like an extended family."

The teens nodded, eager to divert attention away.

"Look at the youth today—fleeting happiness and loneliness. They have a problem for every solution. Always looking for a return in exchange for their time." His glance swept across the room. Many heads nodded in agreement.

As if to prove his point, he added, "Look at you, son, the evening has not even started and you are wondering how you will benefit. Just learn to feel the moment—to live in it, to revel in it- not to rebel in it." The Hakawati bellowed with passion, making a fist and tapping his heart as the crowd cheered.

"Son, and to all of you"—he looked around—"we need faith to be happy. The belief that there is a higher energy to help us when we feel that everything is lost. It is only faith that will ease our burden and help us carry on through the darkest moments."

Pointing to the boys, he said, "Let me tell you a real story tonight. This story has been told in many places in different versions, but the message is the same." The

Hakawati took a sip of his kava, adjusted his shawl, and began:

> A group of young mountain climbers
> had all come together for a difficult
> trek. They wanted to climb the mighty
> Hindukush Mountains that spread across
> India, Pakistan, and Afghanistan. Their
> instructor, Zubair, a mature ex-army man,
> had years of experience in the area. The
> boys were going to climb Tirich Mir—the
> highest peak of the Hindukush. Majestic
> at almost 7,500 meters above sea level, the
> view from its peak was like looking down
> from heaven. Along the route are many
> smaller, but stunning peaks, like Noshak,
> Istor-O-Nal, Saraghrar, and others.

The Hakawati waved his hands before continuing.

> With heavy backpacks and high
> energy, the boys started their Trek,
> passing the Chitral Valley. After a few
> hours of walking over rough terrain, they
> were tired and desperate for a hot meal.
> The boys looked out for the mountainside
> cafés. These tiny native shops were the
> only ones randomly scattered on the wild
> terrain and provided relief to trekkers.
> At one of the clearings, nestled in
> a rugged area, the boys spotted a small
> cottage. Their hopes surged. As they

got closer, they notice a roadside café. A yellow, dim light shone from inside. With a burst of energy at the thought of having hot food, they sprinted ahead. David, the youngest in the group, fell, and Zubair stopped to help him.

As the boys got closer, they noticed that the cottage was old and dilapidated. The windowpane had tiny metal bars on the inside. The glass was stained and cracked and as they reached the entrance, they saw that the door was bolted and locked. It was a rickety old door on loose hinges barely held in place.

The storyteller paused to take a sip of water before continuing;

One of the boys, Ryan peeped in through the dirty, stained window. He could see a few old tables and stools strewn around a small room. A long wood bench was against the opposite wall. The counter held glass jars filled with cookies. A wicker basket on the table held some Arabic nan wrapped in a linen cloth. He saw a tiny old fridge in the corner near the bench. Behind the counter was a long table with a metal top that had a shawarma maker.

Just the very sight of the delicious food through the window made the boys

ravenous as they waited for Zubair and
David to join them.

Zubair walked over with David
limping behind. One look at their tired,
deflated faces told him that the shop
was closed. He felt sorry, but there was
nothing he could do. He said, "Boys, let
us rest here for a while and continue on
our way."

Ryan said, "Sir, I can easily break the
lock. It is old and rickety. We can make
our own tea and sandwiches."

Zubair thought for a second and
said, "Sorry, can't let you do that. It's not
right." The other boys joined in pleading,
"Sir, it's not like we are going to steal.
We will make our own meals and leave
money for whatever we eat."

The storyteller paused again and asked, "Have you
ever tried to say no to a teenager? You will fail." The
crowd laughed as he resumed.

Zubair, the coach, was outnumbered,
and he reluctantly agreed. It took Ryan
less than sixty seconds to break the
bolt and open the rickety latch without
damaging the door, which made Zubair
wonder if they had already fiddled with
it while waiting for him to reach them.

The boys went in and divided chores
among themselves, making sandwiches
and tea. Once everything was ready, they

gathered around the tiny tables and ate in
delight.

Zubair sat on the bench facing the
door, hoping the owner would turn up,
as he was uncomfortable with what they
had done. Ryan brought over a hot cup of
tea, a shawarma, and a plate of biscuits
to him.

The moment he sipped the tea and had
a bite of shawarma, Zubair felt so good
his worries disappeared. He had forgotten
how satisfying and luxurious a good hot
meal was. He grudgingly admitted that
this was exactly what they needed.

When they finished, Zubair took out
some money and left it on the counter
under a cookie jar. He was generous to
leave a bit extra for the door they had
broken. The boys were all from wealthy
families and could afford it.

As Beirut, the last boy to leave,
closed the door, he hesitated. Ryan
muttered sarcastically, "The damage is
done, brother. No point feeling guilty
now." Showing his little finger, he said,
"You go ahead, I want to take a leak,"
and sprinted to the back of the cottage,
out of sight.

In a few seconds, Beirut heard Ryan
calling out to him. He ran to see Ryan
standing over an unconscious man. He
looked up at Beirut. "Looks like he

fell and hit his head. Call Zubair Sir, will you?"

Zubair rushed to Ryan with the boys close at his heels.

"Sir, I came here to take a leak and saw this old man on the ground. He's unconscious but breathing."

Zubair checked him. His pulse was faint. He was still bleeding from a wound on his head. *It could have been more serious, but his turban must have cushioned his fall,* he thought. A bunch of keys lay nearby.

"Get some water, Ryan. Beirut, help me take him to the front," Zubair instructed. After trying without success to wake him up, the boys looked at Zubair questioningly.

"I think he is the owner of the café. He must have closed up and gone to the back when he fell and hit his head. He was lying unconscious all the while as we broke into his shop and helped ourselves," Zubair remarked indignantly. "We can't leave him here. Ryan, Beirut, Kamaal, help me carry him down to the village. They will know where he lives. The rest of you, wait for us here."

It was getting chilly. The other boys huddled in the café waiting anxiously. By the time Zubair returned with Ryan, Beirut, and Kamaal, it was close to midnight. They decided to spend the night there.

Ryan explained to the other boys what had happened in the village. They met some guys in a jeep halfway down who dropped them to the village. The villagers recognized the old man immediately. They helped Zubair take him to the only clinic there. After ensuring that he would be fine, Zubair paid the clinic, and they rushed back.

Early next morning, the team got up and resumed the trek. After weathering hours of challenging terrain and cold winds, they reached a spot a little before where they would have reached yesterday, had they not stayed back for the night.

Zubair was stunned to find that the trail had disappeared under rubble and debris. It looked like there had been an avalanche at that very time they had stayed back at the shop for the night. This was not uncommon here. The boys looked at one another in silence. Had they been on this path as scheduled, they would have been surely hit by the avalanche, and heaven knows what could have happened! This trail was remote and lonely.

They retraced their steps, and Zubair guided them through an alternate path that was more frequented and less challenging.

Finally, the boys reached the summit, absolutely thrilled. The view was worth every ache in their body. It was ethereal and majestic.

On the way back, as they reached the clearing at the base of Saragrar Peak, the boys looked for the café and, sure enough, located it. Zubair wondered how the old man was. To everyone's relief, the café was open. As Ryan opened the door, the delicious aroma of food wafted out to greet them. The boys entered the little cottage and saw an old man with a long white beard in a turban behind the counter. He had a small bandage on the side of his forehead. A young boy was at the table preparing food.

The old man looked at Ryan and smiled at him warmly. "Take a seat, boy, tiring trek, isn't it? But it is worth every ache in your bones. The view is heavenly," he said with a flourish of his hands.

The boys went in and took their seats. Zubair was the last to enter, and he sat on a stool close to the door.

As they waited for their food, Kamaal heaved a sigh of relief. "By God's grace we are safe. If it wasn't for his protection, we may be under that avalanche."

David, just nineteen years old and the youngest, raised his eyebrows and smirked. "Really, Kamaal? We should thank Sir Zubair and not an invisible man in the clouds!"

Ryan agreed. "Kamaal, the problem with us humans is that we do not like to take any responsibility. We conveniently throw everything on God without any proof."

Arif snapped at David, "You can't be so arrogant to question God's presence. There are many things beyond our understanding." The discussion turned into a full-blown argument.

Zubair cleverly stayed out of it, enjoying his tea and the lovely Persian music playing inside the café.

As the argument heated up, the old man refilled their sandwiches and interrupted, "Boys, if I may, shall I say something?"

The boys waited for him to continue. "My name is Mirza; I have spent my entire life here in this village among the mountains. I have seen many storms and winds, extreme cold with no electricity or water, but we have managed to sail through it all with God's grace.

"All of you I'm sure, are more educated and experienced than me with the world. I will not judge whether you are right or wrong, that is totally your prerogative, but I will say one thing with full faith. God is definitely there. I have personally seen his grace and kindness."

David questioned, "Sir, have you seen God?" Mirza nodded vigorously. "Yes, oh yes. A few days back, the devil took hold of my day and God sent his angels to help."

Zubair's curiosity aroused, he moved a bit closer to hear the conversation.

Mirza continued, "Last week, I was here at the shop going about my daily work. Late afternoon, I felt weak so I decided to close and leave early. I came to the back to collect some wood and I remember hitting my head on the ground.

"I have absolutely no recollection of what happened next. The doctor told me that I was lucky to be brought there on time. The villagers said that I had fainted and a group of boys brought me to the doctor and even paid for my treatment. I am sure that if no one had found me that evening, I would have died." Mirza looked at the boys triumphantly, as if he had proven his point.

"That is not all. The next morning, the doctor allowed me to go home. My old mother was worried sick. The moment I reached home, she ran out to see me and slipped and fell, breaking her ankle.

"Nadeem here—he pointed to the boy at the counter— took her to the doctor.

She had to be admitted so Nadeem came back for money.

"I forgot my pain, and I was only concerned for my mother. I came here to take some savings I keep.

"As I neared the shop, I noticed that the latch was broken. I was horrified, my heart sank as I thought someone robbed the store. I asked Allah why he was testing me so much.

"I went in nervously. Nothing was broken or taken, but I saw that a lot of food was missing. I didn't care about that, if some poor soul needed it, he can take it with my blessing."

Mirza looked at the boys again; they were silently eating.

"I searched for the jar, it was still there under the counter, but there was not enough for the doctor. I prayed to Allah to help and that was when I noticed the money, folded neatly, under a cookie jar." Mirza's eyes widened.

"You see, sometimes when things look broken from the outside, there is something better waiting inside. The shell has to break to let the fledgling out because its time has come."

Mirza *jaan* turned to David and shaking a finger at him, said, "*Tifli* [my child] keep your mind open to let the light in. Moonlight touches the sky from horizon to horizon. How much of it enters your room depends on the size of your windows!

"You cannot climb the mountain easily if you carry too much weight, can you? You have to be very light so the weight doesn't pull you down. You cannot enjoy the mesmerizing beauty of the mountains if you take each step with a heavy leg.

"Such is life, my boys. Don't carry the burden of doubt and dread throughout your life and hope to enjoy the journey. Have faith and believe that what you need will come to you."

As he recollected the story, his eyes welled up with tears. "God is there," he repeated, wiping his eyes with the edge of his turban. "His angels saved my mother and me. He is watching over all of us."

The boys looked at one another in silence and exchanged knowing glances. Kamaal and Beirut, the older boys, agreed with Mirza, "Yes, Mirza *jaan*. Indeed, angels walk the earth among us all the time."

David countered sarcastically, "Hate to burst your bubble, old man. God's angels must have forgotten your address because the people who broke into your shop, the money there, the people who took you to the doctor, well—all that was us, what a coincidence, heh!"

Zubair got up from his seat and said in a firm tone, "Shut up, David, that's enough,"

He walked over to Mirza, put his hand around his shoulder, and explained what had happened. He apologized, saying, "I am ashamed of breaking in."

The room was silent, Mirza was quiet for a few minutes. Zubair looked at his face closely. It had the weathered look of a man who had seen many moons. Each line on his face seemed to tell a tale of some pain, some struggle, yet his energy was warm and contagious.

Finally, he lifted hands to the sky and cried, "Al Hamdulillah." He walked over to David, knelt in front of his chair, took both his hands in his wrinkled old hands, and said, "My son, I am blessed. God has chosen all of you as his angels to help me in my hour of need. That is why you broke the lock and got in. I would be lying outside and may be dead if you hadn't been there. I cannot thank you enough for being a savior to me."

David looked embarrassed. He lifted the old man up gently by his shoulders. "Mirza *jaan*, I am sorry for my rudeness," he whispered.

Mirza put an arm around Zubair. "*Saab*, there is no need to apologize, you have maintained the highest level of morals and principles even in an act of breaking in. Where on earth does this happen?" he joked. "My faith in God has only become stronger now. Please consider today's meals as my compliments to you."

Mirza made his famous special tea for all of them and, while bidding them farewell, said, "I am going to tell my family that I am the luckiest man on earth, God's angels came to me not once but twice."

The boys were thoughtful on the way back. The experience had clearly changed them. Maybe there is indeed more to us than what we see. This incredible energy that binds us to and with each other and with the universe.

The cosmic energy connects the dots and sends us to people and places where we are needed, or vice versa. They are part of a much larger pattern which we don't see.

Back at the hotel, Zubair thanked the boys and wished them luck. He hugged each one of them. "Go on, boys, chase your destiny. Be a hope in someone's life and bring a smile to the lives you touch. But, remember, energy is contagious, both positive and negative alike."

The Hakawati took a long pause and looked at his audience. There was pin drop silence. He was aware that his voice had a profound effect. He smiled, "Yes, it was a special trip that changed those young boys and made them realize their worth, realize the power of healing and helping. Was it Mirza in fact who may have been sent to save them from the avalanche?"

He ended the story with this question thrown at us. There was not a murmur from the room. No one wanted to break the magic spell.

The Hakawati thanked us, rose with a flourish of his long, beautifully embroidered robe, touched his hand to his heart, gave a slight bow and disappeared within minutes.

Sitting there, reflecting on the storyteller's words, the mist in my head cleared, and I could see exactly what I needed to do.

When I returned to London, I would meet the management and offer to resign so that Chris could keep his job. In any case, I was more likely to find another job than he. I had an impeccable record, wealthy parents, and age on my side. Chris would perhaps never be able to get another job and he had responsibilities.

On the drive back home, I shared my story with Rehaan and how the evening had changed my perception of life in general. He listened carefully, "Kian, there is no such thing as a coincidence. Everything happens for a reason, and that reason unfolds at the right time in our lives."

Reminiscence

Each one of us has a guiding star watching us from above.

This star is the soul of someone who loves you, protecting and guiding you. This is the star that connects with your core called conscience. If you tune in to listen to that voice inside you, it will guide you to realize your dreams effortlessly and without fail.

Reminiscence

Walking along the cobbled sidewalk, I stumble on a stone and steady myself. I stop and look across the dark, cool lake—the soft hue of streetlights dancing on its gentle waves.

I love my occasional stroll along the lake after dinner. This was my time to ponder, reflect, and be at peace with myself.

My family is rich, successful, and respected in the community. There is little else that we really needed to achieve in terms of success and material growth. I couldn't ask for more—a wonderful husband and beautiful kids.

Yet these walks alone at night makes me realize that there is so much more to life and happiness than the hollow dreams we chase in this world.

A gentle breeze plays with my chiffon gown as I stroll along the path. The quiet street lit by antique lampposts caressed by big, lush trees. It is a beautiful, dreamy moment of a calm, peaceful night.

I look across at the row of houses lining the length of the lake. Quaint, pretty manicured gardens glisten in the moonlight.

There is some sign of activity in most of the houses— some windows with curtains partially drawn, a few open to welcome the night air in, others with a sheer translucent fabric that revealed the silhouettes moving inside.

I observe the myriad scenes across the lake; a couple lazing on the couch, watching TV; a mother and her three kids finishing a late Sunday dinner; a group of friends smoking and drinking on the porch around a wicker table, listening to the tunes of Kenny G.

I smile softly at the sights I just absorbed, the air filled with positive energy and tranquility. I realize that the routine of life is infinite and unbreakable, be it an ant or an elephant.

I sit on a bench close by and look up at the stars in the dark velvety sky, trying to count them.

This is my moment of peace, of serenity. Nothing compares to this feeling of utter bliss I have as when I gaze at the vast dark sky littered with little diamonds. It makes all the problems in the world appear so tiny and insignificant and I am just a dot in the picture. I wonder what secrets and mysteries lay behind the dark veil of the sky and whether we are worthy of the universe giving us a glimpse into her treasures.

My gaze returns to the stars as I try to count them again. I give up and look for the largest star in the sky.

My eyes fill up as memories of a similar moment in my childhood come flooding back.

When I was about eleven, my father would sometimes take my brother and I on a walk after dinner.

As a treat, he would buy us an ice cream or a chocolate bar and we would sit on the bench, counting the stars.

He often asked us to look for the biggest star in the sky, and when I pointed to one, he would smile and say that it was his father, my grandfather, watching us from above and protecting us every day.

"One day, my little imps, I will be there too, looking after you and protecting you. I will never leave your side, just like your grandpa above, watching us," he would whisper with a faraway look in his eyes.

And as I continue to search, I see a pair of stars close to each other flickering and shining bright. They are not the biggest, but they are the brightest and stand out like diamonds in the sky.

I let out a deep breath. "There you are," I whisper softly, tasting the tears.

I find them at last, looking down on me and shining their light on my path.

I blow a kiss to the two beautiful sparks in the sky. I threaten and plead with them to be there every night when I come looking for them. They flicker faster and brighter in response, as if to say they understood. And then I hear them whisper,

"Child, drop your fear, drop your ego. Surrender, trust, and let go. Believe in yourself and in the infinite powers of your soul because you are a part of the great cosmos and will return to it."

The two bright, shining stars—my father and my mother—have illuminated my path constantly with their love, their kindness, their wisdom and their warmth. I would trade nothing in the world for that wealth of experience in this fleeting lease of time.

The pain of losing both parents, or a loved one, is intense and_unrelenting. Perhaps the wound will never completely heal. But hope, as they say, is the magic potion you need to perform miracles in life.

And as my father reminded me in a dream a few months ago, "My child, I may be dead in one time zone, but I am alive in another."

The departed, they continue to illuminate our path in our moments of darkness and self-doubt.

Yes, I am a dreamer, and I continue to believe in this dream. "For a dreamer is one who can only find his way by moonlight—and his punishment is that he sees the dawn before the rest of the world," says Oscar Wilde.

The Brahmin's Karma–Sudra

Karma in Hinduism is a belief that whatever you do—good or bad—comes back multiplied, and you will have to pay back, either in this life or the next. The consequences of your deeds cannot be escaped.

The *varna*, or the Caste system in India, can be traced back to 1500 BC as mentioned in the Rig Veda. There are four main castes: Brahmins, Kshatriyas, Vaishnavas, and Sudras.

Sudras are the lowest caste and regarded as impure or untouchables. No one wants to touch them.

Brahmins, on the other hand, are at the top—placed so high on the pedestal that no one can dream of touching them.

Though it is constitutionally illegal, the caste system is still widely practiced in India.

The Brahmin's Karma-Sudra

Raman worked as the head of the psychology department at the University of Jordan. He moved to Aman five years ago with his wife, Chandra, and three young children, Priya, Arun, and Gauri.

He hailed from Coimbatore, a small bustling town in Tamil Nadu, South India. Raman used to work as the head of the arts department at the Annamalai University before he was offered a job in Jordan. His elderly mother lived alone in their ancestral home in Coimbatore. His siblings lived in various parts of India.

His eldest daughter, Priya, had completed her higher secondary exams and had got admission in Symbiosis College, Pune, to pursue her higher studies. Priya was almost eighteen, a tall, beautiful girl blessed with brains and beauty. She eagerly looked forward to the independent hostel life she was about to experience.

Raman decided that he would accompany Priya to settle her in college. Besides, his younger brother lived in Pune. It would be nice to meet him for a few days. Amman was a safe place, and they had many friends at the embassy circles. His wife would certainly welcome a few days alone.

He was a doting son, and he wanted to visit his aging mother first before going to Pune. Priya was not a big fan of her grandma, having lived with her for a few years before she joined her parents in Jordan, but she knew better than to argue with her dad. Anyways, she was an independent, mature girl now. She reckoned that she could handle the grumpy old lady well.

Grandma lived alone in their ancestral home in Coimbatore. Seven of her nine children lived in different states in India. Her youngest son and her daughter lived close by and would visit her regularly. But none compared to her favorite, Raman, her third and only son abroad. Raman was by far the most handsome, educated, and refined of her children, and she was very proud of him though she never showed it.

Raman and Priya landed in Coimbatore late evening. Her father's brother Krishnan was there to receive them at the train station. It had been a long, exhausting journey. They had taken a flight to Delhi first and a train from Delhi to Coimbatore. The drive from the station was almost an hour, and it was dark when they reached home. Grandma lived in a quiet, partially developed and sparsely populated neighborhood. The *kaccha* roads (unfinished gravelly roads) and dim, old streetlights gave the area a ghostly atmosphere.

As the taxi parked, Priya got out and looked at the silhouette of the house. Nothing had changed. The unforgettable scent of jasmine from the bushes around the fence greeted her as she opened the rickety, old wooden gate. The old fence had gathered a few extra chips and cracks.

A small little house stood in the middle of a large plot of land. A few concrete steps led up the front veranda. A worn out *pandal* (canopy held by four bamboo poles) that covered the front porch served as a shade from the sun and rain.

The red tiled roof had clearly seen better days. A few broken, chipped tiles begged to be replaced. The pale-yellow bulb that hung from a dusty red metal shade in the front porch threw an eerie orange glow around. Part of the lawn (if you could call it that) was covered in thick grass and weeds.

Fruit trees and shrubs scattered all over as if seeds got flung around randomly by the wind and the trees grew wherever they fell.

The years seemed to slip back as flashes of memories rained in her mind. She thought of the water well under the shade of guava trees in the far-left corner of the lawn and turned to see it.

This was the place she would visit after dinner on the nights that she felt lonely. She was barely fourteen years old then. Her communication with Grandma was very limited, mostly to food and instructions on what not to do in the house.

Priya had developed a habit of sitting under a tree by the well after dinner. Oblivious to the sharp pinch of stones on the gravelly ground, she would stretch her legs and lean against the wall of the well, gazing at the stars, talking to them, and making a wish on them.

She found comfort in the rustle of leaves, the sound of crickets, frogs croaking nearby, and an odd chameleon running up the fence, vanishing into the darkness. The scent of jasmine wafting from the bushes all around the fence had a soothing effect on her.

She slowly walked to the house as her father and uncle got the luggage out.

Raman's booming voice jolted her back to the present. "*Kanna* [sweetheart], take this inside, will you?"

She carried a small trolley up the path. Raman sprinted ahead excitedly, eager to see his mother. Priya smiled. Her father behaved like a little boy who had come back home. In fact, he *was* a little boy who had come back home!

Hearing the noise outside, the door opened and a small, frail lady shuffled to the veranda. As her eyes adjusted to the dull light on the porch, she gave a faint smile as she saw her son.

Priya was close behind her dad, and she arched her eyebrows in surprise. This was literally the first time she saw Grandma smile. She almost looked humane! Most days she usually had a frown or a scowl—sometimes both.

"Amma, epudi iruke nee?" (How are you, Mother?) Raman gave the old lady a hug, and both started talking over each other. They went into the hall and sat down. After a few minutes, her grandma seem to remember that Priya was there too. She looked at her and said to Raman, "Unn ponnu evalo valandutta." (Your girl has grown so much.)

Raman smiled and signaled to Priya to touch her grandma's feet. This was an old South Indian custom, touch the feet of elders to greet them. Priya obliged. "Epudi iruke, Patti?" (How are you, Grandma?) she queried. Grandma ignored the question and continued talking to Raman.

Priya took her bag to the bedroom and then went to the kitchen to get some water. She never understood why the house was built so haphazardly.

The house had a small entrance hall with a sofa cum bed on one end and an iron cot with a rolled-up mattress at the other, on which Grandma slept. Next to the entrance hall was a bedroom that guests used.

Past these two rooms was the middle hall. This was the main place, as everyone congregated here. Gray epoxy flooring, built-in cement shelves, and a sloping red tiled roof. Rolled-up bamboo mats peeped from an open trunk, and a selection of pillows and cushions of various sizes in another trunk.

This was a multipurpose room. Dining and lounge during the day and a sleeping place at night. Adjoining the hall was the kitchen to the right. A small passage to the left led to the back door.

Along the narrow passage, three parallel clothes lines hung from the ceiling to dry clothes inside when it rained. They were so high that Grandma had to use a special bamboo stick carved like a V at one end to hang clothes.

A tulsi plant (considered holy by the Hindus) enclosed in a square earthen pot stood regally in the center, like a temple commanding worshippers to revere it.

Grandma's day started at the first light of dawn, with a cold bath, after which she wrapped herself in a cotton sari that would go damp, absorbing the water from her skin (she never dried herself with a towel). She would offer prayers to the tulsi, sprinkle it with holy water, and adorn the earthen pot with sandalwood paste and red kumkum.

After this holy area came the wash place—a cemented floor with a large stone on one end to wash clothes. At the other end was a raised concrete slab to clean the dishes. Adjoining the bathroom, in a corner, was a firepit with an extremely large aluminum pot to heat water in winter.

The back garden was more unkempt than the front. Coconut, mango, and pomegranate trees littered the place, but at least it had a proper compound wall to give some privacy.

At the far end of the back garden, adjacent to the compound wall, were three tiny rooms without a ceiling. These were the toilets—Indian-style WCs accessorized with a tap and a copper jug. The latrines had rough tin doors that creaked every time it was opened or shut.

Priya shuddered, recalling the few nights she had to go to the toilet in the middle of the night during rainy season. Lantern in one hand and an umbrella in the other, it was eerie as the winds howled and the tin door creaked. She almost expected a gnarly hand to grab her as she closed the toilet door.

She remembered fervently reciting "Om Namah Shivaya" (a prayer) and hastened back as fast as she could. Once, she spotted a small snake scurrying across as the light from the lantern hit the ground. For a few seconds, she froze, as did the snake. She then retreated quietly back and decided to relieve herself next to a tree near the well in the front. From then on, she stopped drinking water post-evening for fear of toilet calls in the middle of the night.

Smiling at the thought of how Grandma would react if she knew that she had peed in the front lawn, Priya picked up a jug of water and two glasses and walked over to the entrance hall. Handing a glass of water to her dad, she sat on the cheap, slippery sofa, observing mother and son. Raman sat comfortably cross-legged on the metal cot holding Grandma's wrinkly hand. Grandma appeared pale and drawn.

It was late, and Priya was tired and hungry. She coughed, and as Raman looked up, she rubbed her stomach. He frowned at her and shook his head. Turning to his mother, he asked, "Amma, can we eat?"

Grandma got up swiftly. "Of course, Rama, I have prepared your favorite sambar, rice, and potato curry. Wait a few minutes, let me warm it up first," she replied, hurrying to the kitchen.

"Priya, why don't you go and help her," pointed Raman.

"I can't, Dad. I have just come from a trip and haven't had a bath yet. She will not allow me to touch anything," she quipped.

"Oh yes, how can I forget that she is a strict Brahmin." He winked.

They washed their hands and feet and went to the hall near the kitchen. Grandma had already laid out large steel plates on the floor. She served hot food as soon as they sat. Raman relished his meal thoroughly. It was almost midnight by the time they went to bed.

Priya slept soundly, drained by the long journey. She woke up the next morning, a bit disoriented. Her brain was fuzzy, and she couldn't recollect where she was. The strong smell of incense sticks floated in through the partially open door, jogging her memory. *What a long way from her cozy, luxurious home in Amman just two days ago,* she thought.

As she looked through the metal bars from the window in her room overlooking the front porch, she saw a buffalo grazing outside the fence and realized how utterly different the two worlds were. She glanced at her watch. It was 9:20 a.m., very late by Grandma's standards. She jumped, quickly made her bed, and rushed to the bathroom to freshen up.

Feeling good after a nice hot bath, she walked to the kitchen. She could hear laughter and loud voices. The smell of freshly brewed coffee greeted her. She saw Uncle Krishnan and her aunt Viji, Raman's younger sister. Both of them lived in different corners of Coimbatore. Grandma was busy preparing breakfast.

Viji looked up as she entered. "My little girl. Aiyo, you have grown so tall and beautiful!" she exclaimed and rushed to give Priya a hug.

Viji was about five feet tall, and Priya towered over her at five feet nine inches. She liked this aunt. She was pleasant and fun. Viji lived with her husband's family in Marudamalai, a bit far from the city.

"Thanks, *athai*. Neenga epadi irukinga [How are you, Aunty]? You look the same. Haven't aged one bit," teased Priya.

Her aunt blushed and said, "Podi, vennai maathiri vai." (Tongue like butter.)

"Here, *kanna*, have a cup of coffee." Her dad poured a steaming cup of filter coffee and handed her a plate of *wadas* (a deep-fried savory). They tasted delicious though she doubted it was healthy first thing in the morning.

Priya listened to all the family gossip from her aunt about who was having an affair, who made more money, who was unable to have children, blah-blah, and wondered how strong their spy network must be to know so much about everyone's lives.

She observed her dad curiously to see his reaction. He looked disinterested. Gossip irritated him. He was an intellectual who loved to read extensively and liked to discuss a wide range of topics, like politics, literature, religion, and spirituality. He had absolutely no clue what his kids did, let alone the rest of the family.

Priya asked Viji, "*Athai*, I want to see some old temples here. Can you take me?"

Viji gleefully rubbed her hands together like a kid who had been given an important task. "I would love to take you. The Marudamalai Thirumurugan *kovil* [temple], which is near my house, is one of the oldest temples. It is a bit far from here, so you can stay with me tonight. I will drop you back tomorrow." She grinned.

Priya was overjoyed at the thought of going with her aunt. She loved historical places—museums, temples, forts—and to get away from her grandma was a bonus. "*Appa* [dad], do you mind if I go with Athai?"

"Sure, go ahead, *kanna*, I have to take *Patti* [grandma] to visit our relatives. Come back at your leisure."

Raman knew that she had a frosty relationship with her grandma and was relieved that he would not need to play umpire with them in the same room.

After lunch, Priya packed an overnight bag and left with Viji. Taking a rickshaw was a gripping experience. The rickshaw driver probably thought he was shooting for a Rajinikanth film with his reckless antics. Overtaking cars, cows, and buses and almost ramming into a cyclist who showed his middle finger as he tried to avoid being hit. Viji blistered and wagged an index finger at him. Priya laughed throughout the ride and was enjoying it thoroughly.

They finally reached home. Viji lived in her husbands' ancestral home. Nestled among the hills, it was absolutely breathtaking. The house was a piece of art, with large rooms and high ceilings. The ceiling in the main lobby had a beautiful mural from the Mahabharata, the scene of Krishna and Arjuna going into battle.

Viji led Priya to her room. A large, carved four-poster bed took center stage, and the room even had a proper dresser. It was pure luxury compared to Grandma's house. She wondered how they arranged such a wealthy marriage for her aunt and vaguely remembered her dad and mom discussing the negotiations. (Yes, marriage was and still is arranged in Hindu culture.) Viji, though dusky in complexion, is quite charming and attractive. *Though in her forties, she still has a simple, childlike quality about her,* thought Priya. Viji's only son was in Chennai doing his engineering.

Priya needed to freshen up from the sweaty, dust-covered rickshaw ride. Viji had coffee and pakoras ready by the time she returned. As she munched into the mouthwatering pakoras, she heard a booming voice. "Viji, engai iruke?" (Where are you?) It was the first time Priya saw her aunt's husband as he strolled into the kitchen.

He looked at them and smiled. Viji introduced Priya proudly. "This is Raman's daughter. They have just come from Jordan for a few days. I am taking her to the temple, she will stay with us tonight," she rambled excitedly.

"She is welcome," said the tall, dark man with a big moustache on a round, pleasant face. You should go before it gets dark. Take Shankar with you."

Priya later learned that Shankar was his younger brother. He was waiting for them at the porch to accompany them to the temple. As soon as he saw Viji, he came forward and touched her feet. "Epudi manni?" (How are you, sister-in-law?) he asked. He glanced at the tall, beautiful girl next to his aunt and quickly looked away. He was dark and ruggedly handsome, perhaps in his twenties.

"Shankar, this is Priya, my niece. She has just come from Jordan," Viji repeated.

"Hello, Shankar," greeted Priya and wondered how many times she would have to hear her aunt say "Jordan" in the next twenty-four hours.

Priya was awestruck by the beauty of the Marudamalai temple. Set atop a hillock amid lush greenery surrounded by hills on three sides, it was a fine piece of architecture. The pathway to the top was a tough climb of almost nine hundred steps. The temple was built by the Tamil kings in the twelfth century devoted to Lord Muruga, the son of Lord Shiva and Parvati, and the brother of Lord Ganesha.

Standing atop the hill, surveying the vast green forest below, Priya took in a deep breath of the refreshing pure air. She had heard that Marudamalai abounds in medicinal herbs.

They returned home late, tired but pleased with the day. Viji's mother-in-law had cooked a sumptuous vegetarian dinner for them. She was a chubby, good-natured woman curious about Priya and her life in Jordan. She dropped a dollop of ghee on her rice.

"Look at you, so tall and skinny like a stick, a slight breeze will blow you away."

Priya smiled, not wanting to point out that the chubby lady should perhaps stay away from the ghee altogether. After dinner, Priya chatted with her aunt and uncle for a brief while before retiring for the night.

The next morning after breakfast, Priya and Viji bonded as they went on a long walk in the hilly areas of Marudamalai. Her aunt was far more liberal than she expected. By noon, they returned in time for lunch. She wondered how these women constantly kept the kitchen running throughout the day.

After lunch, Viji accompanied Priya back to Grandma's house. Raman was in the hall having coffee and freshly roasted peanuts. Pleased to see his sister, he asked Viji to join him.

Grandma was apparently busy with her evening prayers.

Priya brought out a box of chocolates and gave it to her aunt.

She saw Lakshmi, the maid, on her hands and knees mopping the front porch. Excited, Priya called out to her and gestured her to come in. Lakshmi looked up at Priya and beamed a smile. She pointed to the cloth and said, "*Akka* [sister], I will finish first."

Priya remembered Lakshmi well. They were about the same age. Lakshmi's mother used to work here four years ago, and the little girl would accompany her sometimes. She was a shy, skinny kid who sat quietly on the porch while her mother worked.

Priya liked her. She had obviously taken her mother's job now. It was a natural transition in this caste for the young girls to take over their mother's jobs. Lakshmi came from a caste called the Sudras, or the untouchables. They had the worst life—lowest on the rung of society discarded by everyone.

Priya hated the caste system. It was against every ideology and belief that she cherished.

She quickly went back to her room and took out a few gifts for Lakshmi, who had just finished her work. It was getting dark. Lakshmi switched on the bulb outside and waited for Priya.

"Come in, Lakshmi," Priya called out to her. Lakshmi didn't move; she just waited outside the door.

"She won't come in through the front door, *kanna*," her aunt interrupted, so Priya went outside.

"How are you, Lakshmi? Why won't you come in?" Priya scolded her. Lakshmi smiled shyly and said, "No, *akka*, *Patti* [grandma] won't approve." She was still a skinny, dusky girl with beautiful features.

"Here, I got a few things for you, hope you like them," Priya remarked, giving Lakshmi the bag.

"Thanks, *akka*, no one has ever given me this much!" Lakshmi squealed in delight after a quick look inside.

"Lakshmi, don't you want to go to school?" asked Priya.

"*Akka*, I can't even think of school. That luxury is for people like you. If we earn daily wages, that is blessing enough," Lakshmi said softly with a faraway look in her eyes.

Priya's heart went out for her. "Wait here," she said as she ran in. Raman was still in deep conversation with his sister.

"Dad, can I have some money, please?" Without a word, he took out his wallet and gave it to Priya. Priya took out 100 rupees.

"Here, Lakshmi, take this." Priya gave her the 100 rupee note. Lakshmi's eyes teared up.

Priya gave her a tight hug, saying, "Come now, things will get better. You are just stuck in the wrong place."

After Lakshmi left, Priya stood outside for a few seconds, gazing at her fading figure, thinking what an unfair place the world was.

As she turned to go back into the house, she saw Grandma standing in the middle of the hall with a frown on her face, staring at her. *She must have been there watching me give the bag to Lakshmi,* Priya thought.

She walked in, ignoring Grandma. Raman and Viji were laughing at some joke between them. She was about to sit on the sofa when Grandma said, "Don't sit."

Slightly annoyed, Priya straightened up, walked back to where Grandma stood, and questioned irately, "And *why* not, *Patti*?" She towered above the frail, old lady, who was barely five feet tall.

Flashes of a similar confrontation one evening four years ago came to her mind. Grandma had been enraged that she had played cricket with the boys. She pushed the thought away. She was far too young and inexperienced then.

The atmosphere in the room was getting tense. Raman and Viji stopped talking as they realized that something was not right. They looked at Priya and their mother glaring down at each other as if ready for a duel. They exchanged glances, wondering what they had missed.

"Tell me, *why* can't I sit down, *Patti*," Priya repeated in a louder, firmer tone.

Grandma, not one to take anything quietly, said in a cold voice, "I saw you touch that girl. You hugged an untouchable, Sudra girl. Do you know how unholy it is? You cannot come in or touch anything until you have a bath first."

Priya's head exploded, and her eyes glinted like steel. She stepped closer to Grandma and hissed, "And you think a bath will bring back my holiness; Dad?" Priya looked at her father questioningly. He quickly looked away.

"Being a Brahmin, you cannot even go close, let alone touch them. These Sudras are impure. Get this into your head that Brahmins are the superior race. So go and wash the sin away," snapped Grandma, dismissing her.

There was pin-drop silence. Both Raman and Viji were awkwardly quiet.

Priya laughed sarcastically. "*Patti*, you should thank your stars that it was just Lakshmi and not a boy you saw me hugging! But tell me, who has made us Brahmins the guardians of purity?" Priya taunted, wagging a finger at her grandma.

Grandma turned to Raman. "Is this what you have taught your daughter Raman? She doesn't know how to respect her elders or talk to them. She will be a failure in her life."

"Don't bring my dad into this, *Patti*. Talk to me!" roared Priya. "I am an adult now. You wake up at 4:30 a.m. and pray every day, hoping your prayers will take you to heaven. You are a Brahmin, placed so high on a pedestal that no one can dream of touching you. Lakshmi is a Sudra, so low that no one is allowed to touch her. Don't you see the irony, Grandma? Both of you are untouchables."

Grandma was speechless. Not because of the tirade that Priya pelted out but because Raman was silent. She was hurt that her son did not take her side.

She looked at Priya and realized that the obstinate girl would not back down, her eyes blazing with the fire of righteousness that only the young or foolish have. She glanced at Raman and Viji. Both looked down without saying a word.

"I never thought I would see the day my grandchild yells at me," she said in a quivering voice, wiping her eyes.

This was a bit much for Raman to take. "Enough, Priya, do as Grandma says," he said firmly.

"But, *Appa* ..." Priya started.

"I don't want to hear another word." Raman glared at her, and she knew better than to argue. "Come, *Amma*," he took his mother away to pacify her. Priya looked at her aunt, who shrugged her shoulders as if to say "What to do?"

Feeling outnumbered and overwhelmed, Priya went for a bath, crying, "No one understands the repression of condemning an entire race as untouchables."

When Priya returned, Viji was waiting for her to say bye. "You are here for a few days, *kanna*. Why do you want a rock show? Adjust a bit, you can't change the old lady now," she commented wryly as she gave Priya a tight hug.

Priya smiled and replied, "If I don't see you before we leave, we will surely meet again soon." Her aunt nodded and kissed her.

Priya declined dinner, not in a mood for company. Raman brought her a glass of milk after his dinner.

"Here, *kanna*, I made this for you with honey and saffron. You shouldn't sleep on an empty stomach. Come, sit with me on the porch while I have a smoke."

Priya wished to be left alone but was in no mood for a debate either. She silently took the glass of milk and went to the veranda. The sky was pitch-black. Not a single star on the horizon. The yellow glow of the bulb on the porch only accentuated the darkness. Raman lit a cigarette and joined her. Both of them sat quietly for a few minutes, absorbing the silence.

"My dear girl, you have a short fuse. Haven't seen this side of you, though your mom did warn me!" Raman smiled, trying to lighten her mood.

"Well, do you agree with what *Patti* said about the Sudras?" Priya bristled.

Raman paused for a moment to look at the tip of his cigarette. "No, of course not. I think it is an unfair practice that should have been eradicated ages ago."

"Then why did you not say anything to *Patti*?" Priya questioned.

"Listen to me well, child. This may be the most important lesson of your life," he uttered calmly.

"Throughout our journey in life, the main struggle, frustration, and heartache we face occur when we deal with others—be it family, friends, or anybody.

"The challenge is the gap between our expectations and the other person's inability to match them. We expect people to agree with our beliefs, our opinions of what is right or wrong and get upset when they don't.

"Rather than try to change everyone around, the secret to success lies in one simple awareness."

Raman suddenly stopped and said, "*Kanna*, go get a jug of water and a glass please."

Priya looked at him, puzzled. She came back with a jug of water and a glass and put it next to her dad.

"Pour a glass of water for me," said Raman. Still puzzled, she did as she was told.

When the glass was almost full, Priya handed him the glass. "Why did you stop? Keep pouring," he insisted.

She continued pouring slowly, and when the water started overflowing, she stopped and put the jug down. Raman repeated, "Why did you stop?

"Are you kidding, Dad? I would be a fool to continue pouring when I can clearly see that the glass cannot hold any more. It would be such a waste." Priya was annoyed.

Raman smiled. "Precisely. You have the wisdom to stop pouring water in a glass when it is full because you know it cannot hold anymore. It does not have the capacity of the jug. It would be utter stupidity to even think that you can make the contents of that jug fit in a glass, right?"

Her interest piqued, Priya listened intently.

Raman lit another cigarette. "People are similar. You can only give them what they are capable of holding. They come with different capacities. Most are very shallow with the depth of a teacup. If you try to fill your capacity of depth and knowledge into that cup, you will fail. A few others are like a glass or jug or even a bucket.

"There are some blessed ones who are like a pond or a well, willing to learn, to understand and to give.

"And then there are those rare gems of this world who are born with the depth of the ocean, blessed with profound knowledge, wisdom, and compassion. From these gems of the human race, we learn to fill our individual capabilities."

Blowing out a ring of smoke, gazing at the dark sky in deep thought, Raman said softly, "My child, learn to read people. It's easy to judge their capacity and willingness to understand. Stop when you realize that it is going to overflow. If you master this, no one can stop you from great success." Raman took the glass of water and took a sip from it.

"Your grandma has the capacity of this glass," he said, tapping the glass. Her glass is already full with her past learnings. Unless she is willing to empty it, you can't refill the glass. You see, sometimes you have to first unlearn to relearn. If you try to teach her about caste, injustice, blah-blah, it is beyond her ability to understand."

Priya knew that he was right. Her instincts told her that this simple yet profound piece of wisdom he shared was going to be valuable throughout her life.

He patted her on her cheek and got up, saying, "Get some sleep now. It has been a long day, and be nice to your ageing *Patti*."

The next morning, Priya woke up early, had a bath, and offered prayers.

Grandma came out to the back porch to feed the birds, like she did every morning. She looked at Priya with astonishment and scurried back inside.

"Raman, is your daughter feeling well?" she queried.

"What happened now, *amma*?" quipped Raman from the hall.

"She is praying! Finally, the girl is getting some sense. Nandri kadavule" (thank God). Grandma heaved a sigh of relief.

Raman smiled. "Isn't that what you wanted?"

Priya walked into the hall. "Morning, *appa*, pass me the paper after you finish."

Raman looked up with a big grin on his face. "Made a good impression, I hear." He winked.

"Not trying to impress. I really want to practice what you said last night. The jug of water theory," she retorted.

Grandma walked in with two cups of coffee. After handing one to Raman, she gave the other one to Priya. "Indha, sooda coffee kudi" (Have it hot).

Priya almost fell off the slippery sofa. Grandma had never done this before. "Thanks, *Patti*." She glanced at her dad, who grinned like a Cheshire cat.

"Drink your coffee and help me with breakfast," Grandma added as she shuffled off to the kitchen. Priya smiled. This was rare. She quickly finished her coffee and hurried to the kitchen.

As this was their last day in Coimbatore, Priya and Raman house-hopped to see as many relatives as time permitted. They were scheduled to travel the following night.

The day turned out to be entertaining. Priya met cousins, uncles and aunts she barely remembered or had never met before.

Typical south Indian Brahmin households. Minimal furniture, a strong fragrance of incense in every home. Women in colorful silk saris with jasmine flowers in their hair. The smell of filter coffee omnipresent. Priya noticed that everyone was well-educated. Even Grandma's elder brother spoke the Queen's English grammatically (minus the queen's accent, clearly).

By the time they returned home, it was almost 10:00 p.m. She was ready to hit the bed, tired and bloated with all the food she was lovingly force-fed by her relatives. Nevertheless, she had a bath first, which gained an approving nod and a "Sleep well, child" from Grandma.

The following day was spent packing and chatting with relatives and friends who dropped in to say goodbye to Raman. Priya had a really nice time. Even Grandma cracked a joke. "If you grow any taller, we can't find you a husband. You will have to marry a tree," said she.

After dinner, Priya's uncle arrived to take them to the train station. For the first time, she felt a tinge of sadness as she bid the old, frail lady goodbye. Priya touched Grandma's feet and unexpectedly gave her a hug. Grandma, unused to such a show of affection, patted her on her head and said, "Seri, seri [okay] take care of yourself."

Six months later, on a rainy Thursday evening, the hostel warden knocked on Priya's door. "Ms. Priya, you have a call from your dad. Come down and take it in the office." Priya was surprised. Her dad usually called her on Sunday mornings. She hoped all was well.

"*Kanna*, how are you. Have you adjusted to college and hostel life?" Her dad's voice boomed from the other end. "*Appa*, how come a call at this hour, is all well?" she asked in a concerned voice.

"Can you take a few days off and go see Grandma? Her health has deteriorated, and she is in hospital. I can't leave Jordan this month as the delegation from London has arrived." Her dad sounded tense and worried.

"Sure, *appa*, don't worry. I will check for tickets first thing in the morning and leave on the earliest train," assured Priya.

She was able to book the train on Friday night. She called her dad and confirmed that she would be reaching Coimbatore on Saturday. Raman told her that her uncle Krishnan would pick her up from the station.

The minute they sat in the taxi, Priya probed, "What is wrong with *Patti*, Uncle?"

Krishnan paused. "The doctors say that it is the final stage of stomach cancer." His voice revealed his pain.

Priya looked at him shocked. "How can it be? You can't just go to the hospital and get diagnosed at the final stage! When we saw her, she didn't mention any pain or …?"

"You know how stubborn *Amma* is and how she hates hospitals," Krishnan interjected. "She never told anyone. She used to complain of a stomach ache but said that it was probably acidity and said she felt better after having cold milk.

"We got to know that Lakshmi first found her unconscious on the kitchen floor five months ago. She stayed with her till Amma woke up. Your grandma made her promise not to tell anyone. Her condition deteriorated over the last three months.

"Two weeks back, when she could no longer get up or walk, we insisted on admitting her. Viji is unable to look after *Amma* as her mother-in-law is also unwell. My office refuses to grant me leave so I can only be with her in the evening," Krishnan rambled on.

"I will do my best to ease the burden, Uncle. *Appa* doesn't know, does he?" Priya looked at Krishnan. He appeared distressed and defeated.

Krishnan hesitated. "We haven't told him yet. He said you would be coming, so maybe you can tell him?"

They were all afraid of her dad's temper. Though her dad was the kindest, most generous man she knew, he had a quick temper when he was displeased. His thundering voice was enough to scare most people.

The house was empty and eerily quiet. The pale-yellow bulb cast an ominous glow on the porch as if to spell a warning for the days ahead.

Krishnan carried her bag to the house and opened the door. "Priya *kanna*, there is a tiffin box with food in the kitchen. Have a wash and eat something. I will take you to the hospital in the morning." Krishnan was breathless as he heaved her suitcase onto the sofa. "I will sleep in the hall, you can use the bedroom," he added.

Maybe he should check his heart too, thought Priya.

The next morning, she woke up early and got ready. Krishnan had prepared a simple breakfast of upma and coffee. They ate in silence.

The nursing home was a small, double-storied building about twenty kilometers away from home. Priya doubted that the place was capable of advanced treatments. Grandma had been given a sharing room. The other bed was empty, so it was totally private.

As Krishnan opened the curtain to let some light in, Priya was appalled and saddened to see the small, frail woman on the bed. She was asleep, her face drawn and grey.

"Priya, I have to go to the office. Lakshmi will come soon. You can ask her to get some food from the restaurant. I will see you in the evening." And her uncle left.

Priya walked softly to her grandma's side and took her bony, wrinkled hand in hers. After a while, Grandma opened her eyes and looked at Priya blankly.

"Patti, enna ithu. Unga udambu epudi ivalavu mosama anadu?" (What is this, Grandma, how did you become so ill)

Grandma instantly replied, "eppo vande?" (when did you come) The old lady's wits were still sharp as ever.

Priya sat on the plastic chair by her side, still holding her grandma's hand. "I came last night, *Patti. Appa* was very worried." Grandma gave a faint smile. "Your *Appa* is a good man. He worries too much. I know my time has come *Kanna,* Do you think I will see him before I go?"

Grandma's eyes had the imploring look of a child as she looked questioningly at Priya.

Inexplicably, Priya choked. Tears rolled down her cheeks silently.

She realized deep down in her heart that she cared for this stubborn, intimidating old woman more than she admitted. She admired her resilience and strength. Her life can't have been easy! Grandma was married at thirteen and became a widow at thirty-eight. Without proper education or a job, she raised nine children single-handedly. This alone was worthy of praise.

Grandma saw her tears and pulled her closer. "You are like your father. You have inherited his qualities. Strong, proud, and compassionate, but you have the heart of a child. I know that you will change many lives, *Kanna*."

At that moment, Lakshmi walked in. She had a tiffin with her. "*Patti*, here are the hot idlis you wanted yesterday." She saw Priya and touched her feet with a shy smile. "Aiyo akka, eppo vandeenge?" (When did you come, sister)

Priya was careful not to touch her as she remembered how it upset Grandma the last time. "I arrived last night, Lakshmi," she replied with a smile.

Priya watched in utter astonishment as Lakshmi went over to her grandma, adjusted the bed, and arranged the pillows comfortably around her. She patiently fed Grandma, coaxing her to eat slowly. It was obvious this was not the first time.

After Grandma had enough, she waved her to stop and pointed to the bathroom. Lakshmi gently lifted her. Grandma signaled Priya, who carefully helped the old lady up and cleaned her, thinking how fragile and helpless the once intimidating iron lady had become.

"Lakshmi, change my clothes. I cannot wear the same gown every day," grumbled Grandma. Lakshmi rushed to her side with a spare gown from the table and changed the old lady's clothes. She then gave Grandma her medication. Cleaned and fresh, Grandma looked happier. She fell asleep the minute her head touched the pillow.

Lakshmi looked at Priya and said in a pained tone, "Pavam akka, Patti romba kashta padaranga." (Grandma is suffering a lot)

Crammed with questions, Priya's head was in a surreal place trying to absorb the current events. How did her grandma, who could not even stand near a Sudra, allow a Sudra girl to feed and change her? It was an unimaginable twist of fate.

Was this what we call karma? she wondered. Hindus believe that no one escapes karma. We have to pay for it, either in this life or the next. Karma is the consequence of our actions, good or bad.

Lakshmi looked at Priya's bewildered face and smiled. "I was the first one to find her unconscious at home, *akka*. She was very weak, so after that evening, I would stay with her every day from morning till night, but she made me promise not to tell anyone. When she stopped eating, I had to tell Krishna Anna."

Priya marveled at Lakshmi's nature. The girl had absolutely no trace of bitterness for the way Grandma had treated her.

They exchanged stories about each other while Grandma slept.

Though they were of similar age, they came from different worlds.

Lakshmi's biological father ran away when she was five or six to escape paying back a loan shark. He never returned. Her mother married again. Her stepdad was an alcoholic, and one night, he raped her when her mother was away visiting her old parents in the village. She was sixteen then. Lakshmi told her mother about the incident when she returned. Her mother turned raving mad and chased her stepdad with an ax. Fortunately, the neighbors intervened before she killed him. He ran away with minor injuries, and they never saw him again.

Priya looked at her stunned. "My god, Lakshmi, listening to your life is like watching a film! How are you still sane after all this? My life is like a damp cloth, nothing except school and college!"

"You are blessed akka, Life is like the jungle for me. I have to keep running just to survive."

"I can help if you want to study Lakshmi." Priya knew her words were pointless the minute she uttered them. Lakshmi shrugged. "What will I do in school now? It's too late for me. This is my destiny. I work in six houses to earn enough just to survive."

It was getting dark. Krishnan came from office looking exhausted. "Priya, your father will be calling you at the reception in fifteen minutes." He pointed to the entrance. Priya hurried to the reception and waited. Raman called, and she gave him the entire story. He listened in silence. "How does she look, in your opinion?" Raman asked after a long pause.

Priya told him the truth. "She doesn't look good. I spoke to the doctor briefly. He says the cancer has spread too far to be able to do anything. He is surprised that she handled the pain so long. The best we can do is to keep her peaceful and painless now."

"I can come after four or five days, once the delegation leaves. I will book soon. I am relieved that you are with her at least. Keep me posted," Raman replied.

They went through similar routines for the next two days. Priya and Lakshmi would spend the whole day with Grandma, and Krishnan would take over the night shift.

On Wednesday, four days after Priya arrived, Grandma looked paler.

The minute Priya told Grandma that her dad would be arriving on Saturday, her eyes lit up. She was cheerful and smiled as Priya and Lakshmi shared funny stories and cracked jokes. Grandma even shared a few funny anecdotes from her past. Priya was pleased to see that Grandma looked much better.

She slept soundly after a week of sleepless nights and felt stronger knowing her dad would be joining them soon.

The next morning, Priya waited on the porch. Her uncle didn't turn up. She assumed that he must be either very tired or busy.

Around 9:30 a.m. she saw Lakshmi at the gate. Priya grabbed her bag, and ran down the steps to greet her. Lakshmi looked distraught.

"*Akka*, when I reached the clinic, Krishna *anna* was waiting outside. He asked me to pick you up and get you to the clinic quickly. I hope all is well. Lakshmi flagged an autorickshaw, and they rushed to the clinic.

As they entered the building, her heart began to race faster. She sprinted inside. Her uncle was talking to a doctor in a corner while another doctor and a nurse were by Grandma's side, making some notes.

Priya's stomach turned as she looked at her grandma. Her body was absolutely still. Her face peacefully asleep. She knew instantly that Grandma had left this world. Krishnan caught her gaze and shook his head. She could see he had been crying.

Apparently, Grandma had gone into cardiac arrest early morning. The doctors had tried everything, but she was too frail and weak to cope.

The place slowly started filling up with relatives. Krishnan left to deal with the admin formalities after the death of a person.

Ironically, Lakshmi, the Sudra maid with the help of a nurse, was entrusted the task of cleaning and changing Grandma before they took the body home.

Sudras—the so-called untouchable caste, shunned and demeaned beyond any rationale—are the stepping-stones of society, literally and figuratively.

Though well aware that they could not even dream of being a part of society's inner circle, they stand by, ever ready to support.

Their eyes beg for only one thing in return—a small validation of being included even in the periphery of that circle, the fringes of society, as an acknowledgment of their existence.

As Priya watched Lakshmi draw the curtain to drape a sari on Grandma's body, the famous Italian proverb crossed her mind.

"Once the game is over, the king and the pawn go back into the same box."

Afghan Hawker

You give but little when you give of your possessions.
It is when you give of yourself that you truly
give. And those who have little and give it all—
These are the believers in life and the bounty
of life, and their coffers are never empty.

—Khalil Gibran

Afghan Hawker

Roy Da Cunha worked with the UN in Kabul in the late '70s. He was of mixed parentage, his mother an Indian and father Portuguese. He had been deputed as a linguistics professor to Kabul to teach English to the native professionals. He spoke five languages fluently, including Farsi. He had been in Kabul for the past four years. Roy had two boys and one girl—four, seven, and ten years old.

He adored his wife, Rita, a kind, beautiful woman he had the good fortune of marrying. She stayed at home to look after the family, which was all she wanted to do, and he was happy with that.

Though he had a decent job with perks, his income was just enough to take care of his family. He was a simple, happy, moderate man. He was neither religious nor an atheist. He disliked any form of fundamentalism and was content at letting life run spontaneously without having to rock his balance. He was kind and did what little he could for the poor in his own way.

He liked the Afghans. They were simple, warm and generous with a purity of heart that could only come from living in a place tucked away, untouched and unpolluted by western civilization. This very raw emotional quality that the Afghans possessed was their strength and their weakness. Every action came straight from the heart, impulsively.

Afghans made loyal friends, and one could count on them in any situation. There was an old saying his gardener often quoted, "Afghans are Pathans, if we love you, we can give our life in a heartbeat, and if we hate you, we can take yours in a heartbeat."

Afghan winters were harsh, and this one was particularly cold and mean. Sleet and snow made it difficult to go anywhere except the office. Social outings and long drives were limited or nonexistent. When winter passed and the beauty of spring dawned, everyone looked forward to going out for picnics and drives, especially his wife, Rita.

The first weekend of April, a breezy beautiful Friday morning, Rita was up early to prepare a picnic basket. With three growing kids, it was a big one—peanut butter sandwiches, cakes, brownies, cola, and some beer. With a beaming smile, she brought in a mug of steaming coffee as Roy got out of the shower.

"Come on, Roy, the kids are excited. Get ready fast so we can enjoy the outdoors. Feels like forever since we have stepped out," she said as she placed the mug on the table.

"Give me ten minutes and I will be out, my love," said Roy as he took a sip of his coffee. All set and ready, he bolted down the stairs to his favorite toy—his car.

He had cleaned his old white Renault the night before. It was parked outside, gleaming in the early morning sun. He checked the car again, muttering, "Oil," check, "Spare tire," check, "Water for the carburetor," check. Satisfied, he got behind the wheel.

Rita walked briskly with the picnic basket in one hand, a bag full of snacks in the other as the kids followed. She settled the kids in the back and they set forth on their way to Surobi—a beautiful place nestled by mountains and valleys speckled with tiny villages. Surobi was around sixty kilometers from Kabul City, covering a stunning drive over narrow mountain roads and valleys. The road was treacherous, so the drive had to be slow.

There were hardly any proper road signs to indicate the steep curves along the way. The narrow road carved across the mountains made two-way traffic tricky and dangerous. With the mountain wall on one side and a deep chasm on the other, one had to be a deft driver to maneuver the hairpin bends whose only warning was an obscure signboard that read "Drive slow, sharp curve ahead" about ten feet before the steep drop.

The signboards were invisible at nighttime so one relied on the headlights of the car, a knowledge of the roads and a prayer to get home alive.

It took almost two hours to reach a scenic spot when Roy decided to stop and take a break. Rita spotted a lovely clearing patch at the foot of a small hill overlooking the dark mountains in the distance. Nature had placed a bunch of trees almost aesthetically to make a perfect setting.

The weather was delightful. A slight breeze swayed the branches musically. Rita got out the sheets and laid them on a grassy stretch as the kids played close by.

Roy glanced at the two families picnicking a few feet away from them. *Clearly, they are far more organized,* he thought. The ones closest to them had laid out plastic chairs and sheets neatly. A boy, probably in his late teens, sat on a foldable canvas chair reading a book while his father was taking a nap under a tree.

A blond lady, most likely his mother smiled and waved at Roy as he got out the picnic basket. Roy smiled back and said, "What a lovely day, would you like a beer?" The lady thanked and declined him.

A bit further from them under the shade of a large tree, a young good-looking couple were relaxing on a neatly arranged floral sheet with cushions. They even had a small table with drinks and nuts!

A portable cassette player belted out some melodious Italian music. Roy wondered how on earth it was possible for them to be so organized this early in the day! He chuckled as he did not see kids. Of course that explains it. What a great time they would have. No kids to run after or constantly bark at. "Whoop, I will most likely not see a quiet, peaceful day for a long time. Maybe if I fall asleep, I could have one in my dreams," mused Roy as he dozed off with the sun hugging him.

Roy heard a loud yelp that jolted him back to reality. His youngest son, Paulo, had tripped over a stone. Rita ran over to pacify him. Paulo had a cut on his chin, so she washed it with some water, dressed it with a couple of Band-Aids and bribed him with a chocolate bar. The pain obviously was tolerable as he bit into the chocolate bar with gusto and ran away to play with the local kids, proudly displaying his injury.

By late afternoon, Rita decided that they should wrap up and drive around to see the village.

They entered a tiny decrepit village. Small mud houses dotted the uneven rugged landscape. Kids were playing on the dusty road. Roy parked under a tree, got out and lit a cigarette. Paulo took the bag of sweets and offered it to the kids, who were delighted. A few men sat in front of a tiny mud house under a tree chatting. They smiled and waved at Roy.

"Nothing much to see in this village, this road will ruin my tires," commented Roy as he drove through. Roy hoped that if he drove far enough, he would reach the main road that would take them back to Kabul.

Soon, they left the village behind. There was hardly anyone on the road save a bullock cart now and then and a few old men walking home.

As luck would have it, the car began coughing and spluttering, and it stopped.

Roy got out and opened the bonnet to let the engine cool. He filled the water in the carburetor and waited a few minutes before restarting the car. Half a dozen trials later he still had no luck. The engine would grunt, heave, and give up. The car had to be pushed to start, but how? There was not a soul in sight on the deserted road.

Rita and the kids got out of the car. She held the youngest child while Paulo and Marta tried to help. It was futile. Roy could see it was impossible to start the car this way.

Roy stopped and looked up and down the road. Not a soul around. Dusk was closing in, and the sky was turning gray. He was beginning to get worried. Wearily, as he looked at the road again he saw a figure walking toward

them in the distance alongside a cart. A bit relieved, he
waved, hoping he could get some help. As the man neared,
Roy saw an old dilapidated cart laden with tomatoes and a
donkey pulling it lazily. The hawker ambled along besides
the donkey, occasionally giving the rope a tug and tapping
the beast with his stick. He was humming a Persian song.
He looked middle aged but strong and fit. He was dressed
in long white kurta and pajamas and wore a turban on his
head.

When the hawker got closer, he first squinted at the
car and then at Roy and figured out the problem. Before
Roy could say anything, he offered, "Biather Jaan, Shuma
komak mekhoyin?" (Dear brother, do you need a hand)

Roy smiled and thanked him. "Baale biather, machine e
man band shuda, methonin dast bidin, khawish mekunam."
(My car has stopped, can you give me a hand, please)

The hawker asked Roy to get behind the wheel, and
without a second thought, he let go of the rope he was
holding.

The Afghan pushed with all his might, and in a few
minutes, the car rolled forward, gave one big jolt and a
sputter, and came back to life. Roy heaved a sigh of relief.

Roy stopped the car a bit further down the road, rolled
down his window, and called out to the hawker as he
waited for Rita and the kids to get in.

He thanked the hawker profusely and was about to
offer him some money when, at that very moment, the
donkey, which was ambling lazily and at such a slow pace,
decided to give it a run.

The dumb ass must have realized that his owner was
no longer around to control him. He went galloping down
the road, dragging the cart behind him.

The rickety old wooden cart was clearly not suited for such adventure. Within a few moments, the cart started shaking and wobbled along the road precariously; ripe red tomatoes started rolling down onto the sandy road, getting crushed.

The poor hawker left the side of the car and ran behind the donkey as fast as he could, cursing the ass under his breath, his turban untying and rolling down in the process.

He soon caught up, but not before half his ware of tomatoes was strewn onto the street.

The poor man bent down to pick them off the road while shouting expletives at the beast.

Finally, the donkey stopped fighting, and the hawker gave it a tight whack on its back.

As he looked back at the tomatoes strewn all over the dirt road, his face fell. Roy noticed the dejected look on the Afghan's face and felt miserable.

He instructed his kids to get out of the car immediately and help the hawker pick the tomatoes. They salvaged as many as they could. It barely took them a few minutes. Roy felt terribly guilty and responsible for this mishap.

If the hawker hadn't come over to help me, this would not have happened.

The hawker stood at the end of the road, contemplating what to do next. Roy drove over to him and apologized profusely. He offered to pay for the tomatoes that had been damaged, well aware that the hawker could not afford such a loss. He did not accept the money in spite of Roy's insistence.

The hawker thought for a second, came closer to the window, and looked directly at Roy. "Biather jaan, Shuma injaa mehman astin. As ma komak mehostin. Chitoor pool bigiram as shuma?" (brother, you are a guest of our land and came to me for help. How can I take money from you) "In our culture, we do not charge for kindness. They are not commodities to be bought and sold."

Roy called him back and presented him with the Kashmiri shawl Rita had on her, saying, "Please accept this as a gift." The Afghan took it, bowed, and left.

He drove off slowly, a thoughtful look in his eyes. There was no value one could place on such a pure, clean act of kindness that the hawker displayed. He hadn't seen something like this before. The lack of greed stands tall and truly conquers all.

Roy commented, "No education or wealth could even come close in comparison to what he did, right, Rita?"

Rita agreed. "His actions would be termed foolish by most of us, yet he stayed true to his beliefs."

"Marta," Roy called out to his daughter, "this is a country of nomadic people who live with their heart on their sleeve, for whom relationships could not be bought and sold with money. A proud race for whom hospitality to a guest is almost revered. We can learn a lot about real humanity from these cultures."

The Afghan stranger who lost half his wares because he came forward to help another stranger on the streets of a tiny village tucked far away between Kabul and Jalalabad - who refused to take comzpensation though he was poor, was overwhelming for them.

Marta nodded. "Yes, Dad, I have many Afghan friends who are very loyal and helpful. They would never sell you out for anything."

Further down the road, Roy spotted a roadside café. Everyone was tired and wanted a snack, and he needed a smoke. They parked next to a tree. He kept the car engine idling, as he did not want to take a chance.

A few wooden tables and plastic chairs outside decorated the little shack that was the café. As soon as they got out, a little boy came running to take the order. They sat at the table closest to the car and ordered some coffee, kulcha (biscuits) and milk. Roy asked the boy to hurry it up as it was getting dark. He did not wish to navigate the treacherous mountain roads at night with his family in the car.

As Roy waited for the bill, he noticed the hawker and his donkey sauntering in, both looking exhausted. As the hawker tied the donkey to a tree the little boy ran over and asked him what he wanted to order. He asked the boy if he could give him some water for the donkey first. The boy ran in and came out with a small bucket of water.

In the open air, Roy could hear the conversation clearly; the Afghans talk louder than most people anyway. The hawker asked the boy how much a pot of tea and biscuits would cost. As the boy replied, the hawker delved into the pocket of his kurta and took out some coins and counted them. He then put the money back in his pocket and turned away.

The boy asked him what the matter was. The hawker replied, "Son, I only have enough money to buy food for my kids. I can't waste it on my tea. Please get me a glass of water to drink, God bless you."

At that point, Roy got up and walked over to where the hawker stood. The moment he saw Roy, he broke into a wide-toothed grin and asked if the car had stopped again. Roy laughed and replied, "The engine is still running as we speak."

Roy turned to the little boy and said, "Get some tea and kulcha for my brother here." When Roy asked him if he would like to join them and pointed to his wife and kids, the hawker fidgeted a bit.

Noticing his discomfort, Roy sat at another table with the hawker and chatted while they waited for his tea.

Roy learned that the Afghan was a fruit and vegetable vendor. He went from house to house to sell whatever crops were in season. He did not own the stock. He took them from a wholesaler and was paid a commission on his sales. The Afghan told him that he had two wives and five kids.

When it struck Roy that the tomatoes that were lost were not even his, he was concerned and touched. He asked the hawker how he planned to pay for the tomatoes that were damaged that evening.

The hawker looked at Roy as if the thought had just dawned on him. He brushed it off and said, "*Biather jaan*, I will pay for it in a few installments over the next few days, depending on the sales I make. Inshallah, all will be fine." Even then he did not once mention or ask Roy for compensation.

Roy was curious. He asked him why he did not take the money.

The hawker let out a deep breath and gazed at the donkey for a minute. "The animals are blessed. They feel stress only on two occasions—one, when they are hungry and can't find anything to eat and the other, when they are being hunted."

His gaze turned to Roy. "Look at us. We are so messed up and permanently stressed because we put a price on everything. Peace, kindness, laughter, love —these are not commodities to be bought and sold, yet we made them into one.

"Afghanistan used to be a rich country. We are proud people, we do not like to take anything from anyone. But all other countries come here, wage war, and tell us, 'We will give you peace and you give us your culture, your resources, your faith, and your dignity in return. They take what we have by force and want to sell it back to us. This is the Western thinking. They always buy and sell everything. We don't."

The tea arrived, and Roy poured him a cup as the Afghan bit into a kulcha hungrily. He continued after a noisy slurp of tea. "You remember me not because I helped you; but because I did it without taking anything in return. If I had taken money, you would forget my gesture, as it would become a transaction."

The Afghan downed the last kulcha, thanked Roy, and got up to leave. Roy took out some money and put it in his hand.

The hawker looked at the cash and immediately gave it back to him, saying, "Brother, please don't. I helped you as any decent human being would. I am sure you would do the same thing. It's not your fault that my donkey is such an ass." He winked. "Don't feel bad about it."

Roy stubbornly insisted. "You called me brother, so take it as a gift," he countered. He had learned that this was the only way to handle an Afghan.

The money was much more than the Afghan would have earned in a week. "May Allah be with you always, you are a good man," said the Hawker as he took some change from the money Roy gave and gave it to the tea boy.

His blue eyes carried more burden than the donkey had on its back. Roy wished him well and added that he had to hurry before it got too late.

Rita signaled that there was a lot of food leftover and wanted to give it to the Afghan. She handed over bags of snacks and chocolates and asked the Afghan to give them to his kids.

The hawker blew a kiss to all of them, bid goodbye and pointed to the shawl on his shoulders, saying, "My mother will be delighted," and drifted away with his donkey into the twilight.

On the drive back, Roy told Rita about his conversation with the hawker and the money he gave him. She was equally touched that in spite of the fact that he was penniless and had to pay for the damaged goods, he had not held them responsible.

Roy was in high spirits on the way back. He felt good, enveloped by a rich, positive energy. He commented that he had no idea why he was so joyous.

Rita smiled. "It is the pure joy of giving without expectation."

Roy realized that it was true. The thought that he was able to make a small difference to a complete stranger made him happy. There was no expectation. This joy in itself was a reward.

Roy often recounts the story fondly to his friends in Portugal—the day when a poor, illiterate vegetable hawker in a tiny village in Afghanistan taught him the pure joy of a selfless act of kindness.

Humanity at its basic—simple and unfiltered.

The Last Fortnight

Inspired by a true event, "The Last Fortnight" is a story that could relate to pretty much any one of us, or perhaps every one of us.

"The light that sparkles to give rise to a new dawn are not those of fireworks, expensive gifts, and lavish gatherings. The true light is to enable the destitute and the defeated to have a brief respite from their agony, to lead them from darkness to dawn.

This is the light that will shine long after you leave this world, illuminating your path onto the next—lifting you to greater heights to bestow upon you the ultimate cosmic calm.

We transit this earth as visitors; only the wise use the time well.

The Last Fortnight

The Professor's Note

Of threats of hell and hopes of Paradise!
One thing is at least certain—This Life
flies;
One thing is certain & the rest is Lies-
The flower that has once blown, forever
dies.
(Omar Khayyam)

Despite constant reminders of our mortality, most of us continue to live in denial of the ultimate reality—that we have a transitional phase on this planet and we will leave our body, however much we love it, and nothing can help us hang on, no matter how hard we try.

The time and energy we exhaust in complaining and hankering for things we do not have, ignoring, or worse still, neglecting the things we do have and finally attempting to regain the time and youth we lost -in vain, only to realize that, with time and age, our energies and needs diminish.

So, in the end – that which we already had and discarded is exactly what we crave for.

Such is the curse of mankind, a vicious cycle he seldom escapes from; forever chasing a distant dream ahead to let what he has slip away.

In our youth, we drain ourselves in search of things that would give us eternal happiness while our mind and body decline. By the time we are ready to taste the fruits of our lifelong labour, we have lost the appetite. As we get older, our mind and body do not care much for the material success we spent our lives accumulating.

At this stage, all you want is peace and a small circle of people who love you.

But where are these people?!

Ah yes, you have ignored all those you love in your quest for success. You didn't have time. You thought you could make it up to them later.

This "later" is our nemesis.

The mantra should be "now" and "here." This is all you have; this is all you need.

To cherish life's moments is a non - negotiable asset, those who discover the magic of living the moment will not stake it for avaricious pursuits.

The choice is ours—to make each day beautiful and memorable; or toxic and damaging.

*E*veryone fondly calls me Professor

I must say that I am not just a regular nerdy academic. I love music, drama, sport - I have a fire within that fuels me to learn everything effortlessly. Tall and well built, I am also slightly vain about my looks.

My biggest weakness, I am told, is my inability to say no, which stems from my desire to see people happy, to support everyone who comes to me for help.

I come from humble beginnings and teaching is something that is very natural to me. I enjoy it; in fact, I think I am born for it.

I have traveled the world, lived in many exotic places; from the Middle East to the Far East and have many friends from different religions and cultures all over the world.

From my early teens, my thirst for knowledge set me apart from my peers. I developed a voracious appetite to read any book I could lay my hands on—be it ancient scriptures, religion, science or literature.

Though born a Hindu Brahmin, to a family of priests and academics, my insatiable curiosity of various faiths compelled me to explore more. By the time I was in my mid-twenties, I had an expert grasp of the Bible, prompting the Christian missionaries to invite me to speak at events and lectures. The pastors and nuns (among my closest friends) would proudly show me off, fascinated by my in-depth knowledge of Christianity.

As chance would have it, I moved to the Middle East in my thirties. Surrounded by Muslim friends and encouraged by my curiosity to learn the depths of this old religion, I read the Quran to understand its essence. The imam at the local masjid in Tehran became a good friend and informal after dinner discussions on weekends about various religions soon became a routine for a small group of us.

This completed my study on the three main religions—
Hinduism, Christianity and Islam; or the Trinity, as I like
to call them.

My interpretation of the holy books is simple. There
is one common denominator - one universal message that
all religions have; which is surprisingly the only aspect
that most people overlook and that is; God is love, is
compassionate and divine. All religions extoll the virtues
of being kind and good as opposed to being nasty and evil.

Had we chosen to follow this interpretation and made
it our foundation, we, as a race, would perhaps be in a
better place. But sadly, that is not the case.

Too often we get lost in greed and vanity. Our
insensitivity and self-obsession make the very attention
and approval we crave from those around us, elusive and
unattainable.

We are constantly plagued by jealousy, apathy, and
bloated egos. Relationships buckle under the strain of
these layers.

We believe that when we have achieved everything
that is perceived by society as a sign of success—i.e.,
money, name, social recognition—we will have all the
time in the world to make up with our loved ones—friends
and family.

> That time will never come;
> And deep down, you know it too ….

> The worldly Hope men set their hearts
> upon

> Turns ashes—or it prospers; and anon

Like Snow upon the Desert's dusty Face

Lighting a little Hour or two—is gone.

(Omar Khayyam)

Now, more than ever, I felt the compulsive urge to get this message across to my children. And I have many—not just my flesh and blood (of these I have four) but my students all over the world. They have stayed in touch with me through the years and are like my own. I celebrate their successes and support them in their failures. Their respect and love for me is boundless.

But I need to tell them the secret of true bliss to make the best of their time here.

At sixty, though fit and healthy (or so I thought) I was rushed to the hospital with a cardiac arrest hours ago.

The Professor

The Last Fortnight

Reform

My doctor was a very pleasant and humorous man with a witty disposition.

He had been treating me for the past two years and knew my stubborn, don't-give-a-damn attitude only too well.

My heart apparently had been acting up again. I had a second stroke when I was brought into the ICU four days ago.

The trigger to this perhaps was my excess intake of coffee and cigarettes the last one month. Admittedly, I had been a bit overindulgent (pun intended heh).

I had developed an unhealthy habit long ago. I drank around eighteen cups of coffee and smoked forty cigarettes a day, for the past thirty-five years.

My doctor seemed displeased that I hadn't changed my habits much, even on the brink of disaster.

"Professor, you have miraculously survived a second heart attack. I am honestly surprised that your heart wants to put up with you at all. Why do you want kill yourself slowly and painfully?

If you wish to die, there are quicker, less painful ways that I can recommend," he added caustically.

His tone became serious. "I will be transferring you from the ICU to the regular ward this evening. You will be under observation tomorrow and we shall discharge you the day after. I don't want to see you here again for the next two years at least, is that clear?" he said wagging a finger at me.

At that very moment, my eldest son walked in. The doctor took him aside and they spoke softly, my son nodding vigorously to the doctor's words.

They ganged up on me threatening to leave me permanently in the hospital if I did not change my habits.

I agreed readily to everything they said; I just wanted to go home!

I was thrilled and relieved to be leaving this wretched place. The rooms were clean, the nurses were lovely and the doctors were good. They had nice TV too, but even the best holidays start to get boring after a while.

Thursday evening, I was shifted to the general ward.

I called my beautiful, adorable wife to tell her that I would be home on Saturday. I asked her to prepare my favorite meals—lentils, rice and cumin potato roasted with butter.

"Sure, I will prepare these gladly, but before you leave the hospital, book another room for Sunday. I am sure you will need it when you have another attack from your sumptuous meal!" she retorted.

I assured her that I was fit as a fiddle and she shouldn't worry her little head much.

If I had a choice, I would have left the hospital that evening.

I bantered with the nurses a bit and cajoled one of them to get me some coffee from the canteen (quite pleased that I still had my affable charm). At dinnertime, I ate an insipid hospital meal and informed the nurse that I wanted to sit on the veranda for some fresh air.

The veranda outside the general ward on the ground floor overlooked a pretty garden. It was therapeutic for patients to sit there and read, or mingle, or maybe just dream!

I had bummed a cigarette off the cleaner earlier that morning. I looked at the cigarette longingly. Taking a deep breath, I lit the Gudang Garam. It had a strong, pungent taste and I coughed a bit.

Surprised, I took another puff and coughed again. There was no cigarette in the world that I was sensitive to! Perhaps it was a tad early for me to smoke, or maybe the hospital atmosphere made me nauseous.

I stared at the cigarette before putting it out and pondered if this was a sign for me to clean up and behave.

I gazed up at the night sky littered with stars and felt a sense of peace. For some unknown reason, I felt a bit emotional as well. I guess having been given a second chance made me realise how precious and fragile life is and how easily disposable we are.

I felt a pang of guilt for having put my family through a difficult, emotional period because of my carelessness and stubborn attitude. They deserved better. I needed to take care of myself as much as they made an effort to look after me.

I vowed to follow the doctor's advice religiously. It would no doubt help everyone if I looked after my mental health more, rather than be an obstinate pain in the wrong place.

I went to bed and slept soundly that night. Perhaps the best deep sleep I had in many years!

The next morning, my sons Jai and Samath came to see me. Since I was no longer in the ICU, they brought some delicious homemade food for lunch.

They sat with me through lunch and waited for the nurse to give my medication before leaving. They had to arrange for funds and complete all the tedious formalities needed to take me home the next morning.

I laughed and joked with both of them, teasing them throughout the afternoon. I called my wife and thanked her for the wonderful meal. I asked her to look good for me when I returned home. She sounded embarrassed and feigned anger. I loved to tease her as she was easy bait, even after all these years. I look and feel twenty years younger my love. I will be home soon," I promised.

My eldest son, Jai, was visibly embarrassed as I joked and flirted with the nurse who came to give my medication around 3:30 p.m.

As my sons were about to leave the room, I beckoned Jai. He approached me and I took his hand.

"All okay, Dad?" He appeared concerned.

"Jai," I replied softly, "I know how difficult it has been. I am sorry for being such a pain. I promise not to give any of you reason to complain again."

My fragile emotional state seemed to have carried forward from the previous night. He looked worried as tears welled up in my eyes. The boys seldom see me like this except when it was time for my daughter to leave after her visit.

I patted his hand. "I am fine. Just feel a bit guilty for putting all of you through this."

"Don't worry, Dad, we love you and totally understand what you are going through. Just come home—all will be good again," Jai teared up as well.

"Did your sister call?" I queried. "Can you call her now, please? I want to speak with her."

"Yes, Dad, she called when we were driving here. I informed her that you will be discharged tomorrow. Get some rest now, you can have a long chat with her later. She is planning to come next week, so you can spend as much time as you want with your favorite child." said Jai sarcastically.

I looked at him apologetically. "I don't have favorites, son, you are all equally dear to me." But everyone knew that my daughter was special to me. She reminded me of myself in so many ways.

They left and almost immediately, I drifted off into a deep sleep.

I had the most confusing dream …

I saw my mother approach me and for the first time in my life, I heard her sing (She had never even hummed to any of us, let alone sing)

I was shocked and embarrassed as she sang to a room full of people I hardly recognized. My mother had an awful voice, almost like a croak, which explained why she never sang to us.

The scene suddenly shifted—I was running in the woods being chased by a white panther in the early hours of dawn.

I ran for my life and somehow seemed to outrun the panther. I continued running for miles without looking back for fear that the panther would catch up with me.

I tripped on a branch on the path and fell headlong onto the ground, my chest exploding as it hit the stump of a tree.

The pain in my chest was excruciating.

I tried to open my eyes. I could see the blurry shadow of the nurse rushing toward me with something in her hands.

I tried to focus again and saw the defibrillator she was holding. The next second I could feel the pain of the electric shock pulsating through my entire body as if a streak of lightning had passed through it.

I wanted to tell the nervous, moronic nurse that using a defibrillator was a tad stupid and a bit much for a simple chest pain. Obviously, my chest would be hurting from the impact of the fall, but the shock would make it worse.

I opened my mouth to tell her that if she would just back off and let me catch my breath, I would be fine, but I felt paralyzed. I could not move any part of my body, let alone my lips.

The nurse kept coming at my chest with that insane tool and continued giving me shocks as the doctors rushed in.

I could see as if through a mist. I lost count and sensation of the shocks.

Suddenly, my body felt very heavy. I had the sensation of sinking deep into myself almost to the depth of the ocean and then I went numb. I could feel no pain.

At that instant, every cell of my body felt alive—as if charged by millions of volts of electricity. I had a tingling feeling, starting from the tip of my toes going upward to my head. The nurse sure must have used a powerful shocker!

And just as suddenly, a wave of darkness enveloped my eyes, followed by intermittent flashes of pulsating light.

I must have slipped into a coma, as I felt a calmness envelop and hug me comfortably, reminding me of the time when my mother would hug me tight as a child whenever I was afraid. Her hug would instantly give me the strength and security to overcome my fear.

This calmness gave me the strength and before I passed out, I knew instinctively that there was no need for me to be afraid of what lay ahead;

> The moving finger writes and having Writ
> Moves on: nor all your Piety nor Wit
> Shall lure it back to cancel half a line,
> Nor your tears wash out a word of it.
> (Omar Khayyam)

My heart stopped beating a few minutes ago ...

The Last Fortnight

Release

There was a door to which I found no key;
There was a veil through which I could not see:
Some little talk awhile of Me and Thee
There was—and then no more of Thee and Me ...
—Omar Khayyam

A gentle voice whispered softly in the professor's ears to go to sleep. It was late; he needed the rest, and if he stayed awake much longer, he would not have the energy for the long journey ahead.

When he woke up, he felt vibrant and refreshed, as if his whole body had been supercharged with the mammoth electricity of a lightning bolt! Every molecule of his being was like a powerful antenna absorbing the vibrations around him.

The nurse must have done a damn good job with the electric shock, reflected the professor wryly.

He looked around and realized that he was amongst beautiful, tranquil surroundings. Lush green valleys met his gaze as far as he could see. Soft white clouds glided gently, almost touching the purple hills that were partly hidden by fog. A soothing calm pervaded the atmosphere.

The professor took in a deep breath of fresh air feeling the exhilaration, as he closed his eyes for a moment.

It slowly dawned on him that he was not in the hospital. When had he come here? Where were his sons. He had spoken to them in the morning. Strange that he had drifted off to sleep and woken up in this gorgeous paradise!

Slightly disoriented, he realized that he was alone; he could not see anyone around to inquire. The only thing to do was to wait, or if he was lucky, maybe someone would pass by soon. He selected a spot and sat on the velvety grass overlooking the gorgeous mountains while he tried to piece together a plan.

A few moments later, he heard a crisp, gentle voice behind him.

"Professor?"

The professor turned and saw a man. He wondered how the man got there without him knowing. Surely, he would have—should have—spotted the stranger. The horizon was clear and the view unobstructed from trees or rocks. His brain was muddled.

He surmised that maybe he was too lost in thought to notice. But that could wait; he would ponder on it later. He was just relieved that someone came by.

The professor assessed the stranger. Tall, dignified, surely as old as himself if not older though he looked much more energetic and alive - as if glowing from within.

There was a powerful, magnetic aura surrounding him.

As his gaze met the stranger's, the professor was shaken by its intensity. It was like looking into the windows of the universe and slowly being pulled into the centre of a vortex. Strangely it felt familiar.

Everything about the stranger indicated that he was used to being in control.

The professor was surprised at how comfortable he felt in the stranger's presence.

"Sir, I was wondering …" he trailed off. The stranger's eyes told him that he knew every word the professor was thinking before he uttered it.

"You are wondering where you are and how you got here, Professor?" The stranger smiled.

"Yes, sir, I must have trespassed on your territory, God knows how!"

The stranger's smile widened as the professor cast a sheepish glance at him.

"I can't seem to remember anything. In any case, I have been having problems with my memory the past few months, so it will not surprise me to know I have wandered.

If you would be kind enough to lend me your mobile phone, I will call my son and ask him to pick me up." The professor extended his hand, hoping to get the stranger's phone.

The stranger regarded him gently and offered his hand. "Here Professor, come, walk with me. We need to talk. I don't think you can call your son from where we are. Though you have been here for precisely forty minutes, it is indeed out of the world," said the stranger as he helped the professor up.

Ah, then I can't have wandered far, thought the professor. *I will have a polite talk to humour him and go on my way home.*

"You seem to know me? Pardon me Sir, but I don't remember meeting you before. My sons would be worried to death to know that I am missing. I really need to let them know."

"In time, Professor, in time. All your questions will be answered. A little patience helps. Your sons already know- and yes, you know me, but you haven't met me before," replied the stranger.

The professor was not in a mood for riddles, but he decided not to argue. He wanted the stranger to finish talking as he was impatient to get home.

"You know me because we are part of the same cosmic energy. The confusion you feel is natural. You will eventually understand and accept the changes you are about to experience.

"You are one of the gifted ones, Professor. You have an abundance of everything," the stranger nodded approvingly.

The professor looked at him perplexed. *Apart from knowledge and (foolish) generosity in abundance, he had little material success; penniless to be honest. The first part clearly explains the second part. He laughed, "you certainly don't know me then, Sir."*

As if he read the professor's mind, the stranger interjected, "I don't mean wealth, surely. You will have no use for it here anyway. You are gifted with a depth of compassion and wisdom but you have one problem.

You are far too sensitive. You lack the ability to detach yourself from people and situations around you - this causes you pain."

He paused before adding, "It is important to first realise, that all problems are not yours, professor. You must teach people what you know and let them walk their own path. Though you are benevolent and have changed many lives, a slight amount of self-discipline would have enabled you to do more."

The professor was getting annoyed. Whoever this old man was, he didn't have a right to assess him.

"Only two people are allowed to criticize me, one is my mother and the other is myself," he mumbled loud enough for the Stranger to hear, "Sir, I admire your amazingly accurate assessment of me, can we just agree that I am not perfect and move on? If you would kindly show me the way back, I will be out of your sight before you know it," he asserted in a louder tone.

The stranger regarded the professor sympathetically and said slowly, "My dear professor, if I could send you back, I would, but I cannot. No one who comes this far can reclaim their body after meeting me.

"In the lower levels, the soul first meets one of my angel guides. There are rare cases, but at that stage if the guide decides, the soul can be sent back for a short while. You are on a different realm professor."

The professor tried to push back the realization of what he already knew in his subconscious. Flashes of memory slammed into his mind. He remembered his body getting heavier and ah, the weird dream he had.

"Professor, your heart stopped beating fifty minutes ago. Your physical body is useless now. It cannot accept you back. Your mind and spirit are here with me. I am the guardian of the afterlife," he declared.

The professor tried to stop himself from reeling back as the words hit him. He sat down. "But how can it be? I can see you as clearly as I can see myself. Surely if I am dead, I would be unable to see anything, isn't that right, sir?"

The guardian sighed. "Professor, you see me in human form because that is what you are trained to see. Your mind is taught to put a shape, face, structure to everything; to make it real. You do not believe what you cannot touch, feel, or see. You are in transition now," he continued. "In time, you will realise that we are formless energies of light and can take any shape we want to."

The professor still could not absorb all this. "Sir, if I am indeed dead as you say and we are chatting away here, how come we are alone? I don't see any other soul and from what I know of our world, myriads die every hour. Have they all gone to the underworld and I am the only holy soul in heaven here, eh?" he retorted.

"Ah my dear Professor, I see that your wry wit and sarcasm haven't been affected!

First, there is no hell or underworld. That is a complete concoction of the human mind. There is however, an astral world. Sure, millions die every hour. Their souls are in transition at various levels. They are being received and inducted by various guides at each level.

"Let me explain in simple terms. You see, professor, we have various levels here. The souls who have departed and are capable of a level 2 cannot be inducted to a level 3 or 4, as it will be difficult for them to cope with the expectations of that level. It is beyond their current capacity. They will graduate each level when they are ready.

"You, on the other hand, have a head start. You have utilised your life on earth in an exemplary manner. You have touched many lives in a meaningful way. You have been noble, kind and generous. Did you say that was foolish, professor? The guardian smiled.

The professor fidgeted with all the praise he was getting.

"Professor, it is true that you gave wholeheartedly, without restraint or regret – but did you ever wonder how things just fell into place for you all the time?

The professor knew this to be true. Though he made very little wealth, he was able to help thousands of people realise their dreams because things would always fall into place magically. Someone would come forward to assist, things would turn in his favour as he tried to get those free surgeries for the poor, jobs for the discarded minorities, homes for the orphans... He could not recollect even one person that he had to turn away.

The guardian articulated with a sweeping flourish of his hands;

"It is because we direct our energies to bolster your efforts. We are constantly observing gifted souls. The predicament is that, we know they are gifted, but we can't support them unless they realise it too and once they begin using this gift meaningfully, we send our energies to strengthen them.

This is the only growth, the only achievement that matters here. For most souls, this awareness alone will accelerate the level they transcend to once they depart their body."

The professor was overwhelmed and a bit embarrassed, "Sir, I thank you for your kindness, but I am not without flaws. I don't deserve all that you have said of me."

"Everyone is flawed. Even our angels here make mistakes. Earth was created as a place to make mistakes. The great force you call nature also makes mistakes. The human race abounds in them. What is precious is to keep your core free from decay.

"Compassion, Professor. One of the reasons you are with me here, on the seventh level is your ability to filter the layers of greed and arrogance and keep your core humble and compassionate.

This is a much higher plane and once you have come to terms with your transition, you can do a lot more to help the disturbed souls on other levels."

The professor let it all sink in slowly.

"The astral world is in some ways similar to the earth. Souls inhabit various levels- some in the infancy of their growth and there are those who progress rapidly to various advanced levels, to become masters. These masters form a council and are the caretakes of the astral world.

"There are nine levels in total. The ninth and the last level is the highest order. When you reach there, your mind and soul will merge with the cosmos. You will not return in any form or shape—be it human or spirit. It is the ultimate peace and oneness with the universe.

"There are strict laws and disciplines in this realm, professor. No one is above the universal law of justice, including me. There are no favours and bribes here.

"Once a soul passes the fifth level, there is very little supervision needed. They set their own boundaries and goals and seldom stray. They graduate to the next level through self-discipline and selfless work. Their job is to assist and guide all other junior souls. I must warn you that there are good and bad souls here too, professor."

The guardian paused and looked inquiringly at the professor. "I don't need to elaborate, do I?"

The professor nodded.

"My dear Professor, most people do not realize that how well they cultivate their inner being determines their next experience. If they have chosen a life of upliftment, their soul will automatically enter a higher level.

"Then again, if you are stuck in the negative sphere of violence, abuse and greed, you will pass through an endless cycle of births and deaths. it will take you many lifetimes to reach an elevated spiritual plane."

The professor agreed, "Yes sir, I am a strong believer in karma or consequence. I am aware that if we lead a life of abuse, deceit and hatred, we have automatically chosen to enter the basic astral level from where we will return to earth, most likely at the receiving end of all the negative energy we delivered in our last life."

The guardian was pleased that the professor was so aware, but then, any soul who entered his realm directly was already elevated.

"Very true, Professor, maybe one day you may graduate to become one of our guiding angels;

And stop calling me sir. It's just human vanity—it is meaningless," chuckled the guardian.

"But now, before we proceed further, it is my duty to make you aware of what you will do and where you will go. Is there anything you wish to say?"

If anyone could handle death, it was the professor. He was a spiritual man, not a religious one. He was not afraid of dying. It was something he had always expected and respected as an integral part of man's existence on earth. He considered death as a new, greater beginning.

But even he could not let go abruptly.

"I have one request," the professor hesitated. "Can you give me a little time, please? Not long, a few weeks or maybe even a fortnight?" The professor turned to the guardian, his eyes begging him.

"Why?" the guardian asked.

"I want to wrap up some unfinished work, say goodbyes properly and leave with one lasting happy memory," replied the professor.

"You, of all people, are among the more evolved ones, Professor, but even you cannot resist the urge to cling on!" observed the guardian.

"This is the weakness of the human race—you are so busy squandering time, chasing fame and fortune that you lose sight of the only truth. A meeting with me - it is non-negotiable. When it is your time to visit me, you cannot avoid it. I always win.

"Mankind has not yet learned to cherish the time given. Neither has he learned to let go gracefully when the time comes. For all his vain intelligence, he lacks the basic wisdom and contentment that is the gift of the other species. The root of grief is greed. Letting go is difficult because he has not learned to curb this.

"All other species have a much shorter life span, yet they are happier. They don't fight or complain when I take them.

"Is it not wiser to make peace with death and live each day to its best?

The professor looked away, a bit ashamed of himself. The guardian was right. Like most people, he had believed that his end would not come so soon. That he had the time, to write his script the way he wanted to and practice his goodbyes perfectly when the moment came for him to go.

Procrastination appeared to be his greatest enemy now;

"Wish I hadn't told my wife to wait when she wanted us to visit our grand-son in Canada. Wish I hadn't stopped my daughter when she wanted to visit me for a few days, I asked her to wait for the long holidays instead. Wish I had talked to my students who desperately needed my advice. I needed to find a way to help, somehow!"

His mind racing restlessly, his chest heavy with sadness, he looked imploringly at the guardian begging for a solution;

"Yes, I am aware you want to help others, professor, which is why I will share a secret. Every soul is disoriented and too attached to everything around when they leave the body. They meander on the earth for a while. It usually takes a fortnight for the soul to accept the truth and be ready to exit permanently."

He looked at the professor gently, "So here you are, you have a fortnight. You will be able to see and hear everything around you, able to travel anywhere at the speed of light, be at any place you think of it ... So, go and find a way to finish what you have to before the fortnight is over.

"But there is a catch —*you won't be able to get back into your body.* You are pure, powerful energy, the truest form of your soul now. Make haste. And knowing you professor, you will find a way. We will meet again soon."

The guardian vanished like a flash of lightning.

After he departed, the professor hastened to reach out
to his loved ones; to try and finish everything he had left
unfinished in the last sixty years - in one last fortnight.

Make the most of what ye may yet spend.
Before ye too unto the dust descend;
Dust unto dust to lie with dust
Sans singer, sans song, sans wine and sans end
(Omar Khayyam)

We are all holders of multiple destinies.

The choice is completely our own. It has nothing to do with fate.

The easiest way to explain it is with this analogy;

Your father has given you keys to three houses and says that whichever one you choose is yours to keep.

The first house is nearby— very easy to reach, but simple and basic. The second house is further away. The path is long and difficult, but the house is more beautiful. It is perhaps something from your dreams. The third house is very far. The path is lonely and long, with twists and turns. It is very tiring, maybe even dangerous at times. But once you reach there, you find that nothing compares to what you see; the house is exquisite- it is more than anything you ever dreamt of.

You have the choice to go to the house you want to – the keys are in your hands - That is your destiny….

The Professor

Thank you

I cannot close this book without acknowledging the contribution of the most important figures in my current existence.

To Sanjana - my beautiful, kind and sensitive daughter who is likely to overtake me with her generosity and compassion to everyone around her and my equally kind, wonderful husband Jonathan who has unconditionally supported me in everything I have endeavoured to do. I am grateful to both of you for putting up with my quirks and for inspiring me to turn my dreams into reality.

I am indeed blessed to have a large family that spans 3 countries, across different religions and different races. These are my extended family of our NGO Healing Lives, who have contributed to make me the person I am today, and though I can't name each one of them, they form an integral part of me – my heart.

Together by my side, each member of healing lives and our partners, toil tirelessly and selflessly to provide whatever help and comfort we can to the remotest, forgotten villages and slums in India, Kenya and Bangladesh. They are truly the epitome of hope and reaffirm our conviction that mortal angels do walk among us.

& finally, to my brothers and my sister who hold a special place in my heart;

My love and concern for all of you does not need attestation....

Let us continue to heal – One life at a time....

159

HELP US HEAL ONE
LIFE AT A TIME

Healing Lives is a self funded humanitarian foundation operating extensively in Kenya, India and Bangladesh. Our main areas of focus are education, basic healthcare, agriculture & women empowerment.

However, due to dire needs we launched emergency relief and aid of food & basic supplies since 2017 in times of floods and droughts.

Our mission is to grow and expand the Healing Lives family no matter which part of the world, which color, religion, or culture they belong.

To bring back the "HUMANE" side of Humanity to every life we touch.

---

healonelife   Healing Lives
HealingLives_HL   healonelife

www.healing-lives.org | info@healing-lives.org

Jani
Viswanath Phd.

Born to a traditional Brahmin family in South India, Jani spent her formative years in Kabul, Afghanistan. As a daughter of an educationist, her extensive travels and exposure to multiple cultures and countries have shaped her personal growth & beliefs. She speaks 6 languages fluently.

After a long successful corporate career in Brand development, buying & Retail, Jani founded the NGO 'Healing Lives' which she is totally devoted to.

Jani's other passion is her Art. She enjoys painting with knives and blades on oil colours giving her art a raw textured beauty.

She is a recipient of art awards from Spain, Italy & New York. She credits her late father for being an exceptional, compassionate human and a role model for encouraging her to give back to humanity Jani's writing is inspired by the connection she feels with the simple, beautiful people she meets in remote places during her travels. These people albeit flawed are inherently kind and warm and they form the core of her characters in her stories.

Jani currently divides her time between Dubai and Portugal and travels extensively to oversee the work of her NGO.

www.healing-lives.org | www.janiviswanath.com